CEREMONIAL SPIRIT POSSESSION
IN AFRICA AND AFRO-AMERICA

SUPPLEMENTA AD NVMEN, ALTERA SERIES

DISSERTATIONES

AD HISTORIAM RELIGIONUM PERTINENTES

EDENDAS CURAVIT

C. J. BLEEKER

VOLUMEN QUARTUM

LEIDEN
E. J. BRILL
1972

CEREMONIAL SPIRIT POSSESSION IN AFRICA AND AFRO-AMERICA

FORMS, MEANINGS, AND FUNCTIONAL SIGNIFICANCE FOR INDIVIDUALS AND SOCIAL GROUPS

BY

SHEILA S. WALKER

LEIDEN
E. J. BRILL
1972

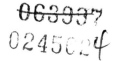

ISBN   90 04 03584 2

„Et le corps de ballet . . . est l'image du monde entier"
Marcel Griaule, *Dieu d'Eau*

TABLE OF CONTENTS

PREFACE

Reality is complex, and the first task of any scientist is to delimit specific problems within a restricted field of data (Max Gluckman).

The above words have especial relevance to the subject matter of this book. For in writing about the limitations social scientists impose in time, space and aspect of phenomena studied, Professor Max Gluckman (*Closed Systems and Open Minds: the limits of naïvety in social anthropology*, 1964) rightly insists such closure assumes that there is a system of interrelations which can be considered separately from the rest of reality. And that assumptions made about aspects of the phenomena which are studied by other specialists are often "naïve". Rarely in the social science literature, we are baldly reminded, have the observations and analyses of events set down in the writings of social anthropologists been viewed by scholars in other disciplines, where different and possibly contradictory interpretations of these phenomena might unfold. *Ceremonial Spirit Possession in Africa and Afro-America* is, in large measure, the response of a promising young scholar to Gluckman's perceptive observations.

For the above, and other reasons which I intend to set down, this book is of interest to me. And I have little doubt that my colleagues in social anthropology will concur with my judgment that the uniqueness of the analytical approach Walker has adopted in this study of spirit possession fills a neglected gap in our knowledge about this aspect of religious behavior. But prior to that I take space to state my pleasure at being invited by Sheila Walker to write the foreword to her first published study.

First off, Walker eschews many of the common concepts social anthropologists, and behavioral scientists generally, have applied to the analysis of spirit possession, and in this approach she ploughs fertile ground. Culture, society, social structure, process, symbolic interaction, and similar terms, concepts and models which usually furbish the standard tool kits of social anthropologists are often inadequate, as we are sometimes reluctant to admit of our craft, to provide satisfactory explanations of the phenomenon which forms the subject matter of this book. Valuable as such theoretical equipment is to the analysis of certain temporal and spatial events, a rounded understanding of spirits, mediums and clients in the religious context of possession cults defies the limitations of closure imposed by cultural and social structural analyses. Close on to that is a second interest of mine in this study. It is an initial attempt, insofar as I am aware, to interpret a wide range of ethnographic descriptions of the behavior of possessed persons in states of trance by utilizing theoretical insights drawn from the psychological and biological sciences. Walker's interpretations are not easily led astray by those studies which have dealt with the ritual therapeutic treatment of possessed subjects, frequently viewed as suffering from psychic disturbances (e.g., Ari Kiev, *Magic, Faith and Healing*, 1964).

Social anthropological writings on the subject of spirit affliction most always express naïvety about the neurophysiological and infra-structural elements involved in possession behavior. Perhaps it could not be otherwise. For the scientific training of the authors led them towards arriving at explanations of the social and cultural rather than the biopsychological expressions of human behavior. I note here that Walker's training has spanned both fields of theoretical and analytical concerns in the behavioral sciences. Thus equipped, she is capable of drawing several distinct but overlapping analytical boundaries, and in each of these fields she makes an exhaustive interpretation of the ethnographic materials at hand.

One such boundary is geographical and cultural. Here we see that similarities in the social environments in large part attribute to the strikingly close correspondence of possession cult behavior between Afro-Americans in the New World and Africans in West Africa. Social environmental conditions facilitated the retention of certain African religious cult themes presently observed in Afro-American cultures; these survived among the latter, though somewhat modified, despite the black diaspora. A second analytical boundary defines, for purposes of interpretation of possession cult behavior, a working concept of religion. In this sense, religion is understood to mean the way man creates a coherent system of cosmogonic interpretation of the natural and supernatural worlds; and in its expressive form of public ceremony, as possessed persons display manifestations of their spiritual presence, it solidifies the human collectivity. Moreover, the sharing of similar spiritual experiences is seen to provide a common basis for the habitually possessed to create socio-religious networks of interaction which cut across other ties of social alignment, thereby linking together disparate individuals and groups into more meaningful sets of primary social relationships. From this characteristic feature of what might be called "the social organization of the possessed", Walker goes on to establish yet another overlapping boundary for analysis and interpretation. At this point, discussion centers on the cathartic effect which public rituals serve for the structurally deprived in the socially and economically stratified societies of the Caribbean, Latin America, and Africa. Here, of course, cannot avoid being brought to mind the rebellious rituals performed by women towards their menfolk, and subjects towards their king, which have been described for the Zulu (Max Gluckman, *Rituals of Rebellion in South East Africa*, 1958), and Swazi (Hilda Kuper, *An African Aristocracy*), however, these ceremonial rituals of southeastern Bantu peoples fall outside the principal ethnographic scope of Walker's concern.

Space permits me to only touch upon the few socio-cultural levels of Walker's descriptive analyses, or "closed systems" to use Gluckman's phrase, that I have singled out for emphasis in the foregone. I cannot take leave of this cursory outline, however, without again stressing the importance of the psychological and bio-cultural interpretations of the data Walker examines, which makes for unusual clarification of the mechanisms of spirit possession.

It is true, of course, that social scientists have not been altogether naïve about the biogenetic endowment of various groups of human beings. It is generally accepted, though without empirical verification, that variations in bodily constitution and psychic structure might bear upon the weighty questions of customs, institutions and social relationships, in one context or another. The scientific importance of such skilled knowledge, as an adjunct to examining patterns of culture as related to the structure of social relations, has been stressed variously, heretofore, in the collaborative writing of behavioral scientists, many of such scholars having been deeply rooted in the discipline of social anthropology. Margaret Mead, Abraham Kardiner, Ralph Linton, Cora DuBois, Erik Erikson, Gardner Murphy, John and Beatrice Whiting, Gregory Bateson, all are in this category of scholars to be mentioned. They, as well as other scholars with similar orientations, have dealt in their writing with problems ranging broadly from the cross-cultural determinants of "sex temperament" and group personality to cultural processes of socialization and anxiety behavior. Yet a careful perusal of such works reveals a striking neglect of cross-disciplinary interest in the bio-psychological concomitants of spirit possession; this phenomenon of human behavior, which, as Walker writes, has existed in most areas of the world.

Walker's study of the ceremonial aspects of spirit possession, then, nestles comfortably with those of other social scientists concerned with cultural variability in human behavior as expressed religiously. The contributions both by social anthropologists and physical scientists which have shaped her training are brought home forthrightly through the insights she has been able to bring into this carefully documented and detailed analysis of the behavior of spirit possessed persons. The reader is reminded, as is so often regrettably necessary, that possession behavior is no longer viewed, at least not by social anthropologists, as bizarre manifestations of hysteria, neurosis, or psychosis. Thus Walker joins company with Raymond Firth, Clyde Kluckhohn, Irving Hallowell, E. E. Evans-Pritchard, Seigfried Nadel, and John Middleton, who, through their collective contributions, have enlarged enormously upon our ethnographic and scientific knowledge and understanding of the religious ideas and ritual practices among peoples in cultures different from our own. As senior scholars, they have provided religious detail to the cultural mapping of the social systems of aboriginal American, African, Asian, and Oceanic societies. That task for Afro-Americans remains to be undertaken by such junior scholars as Sheila Walker. Thus, her first study also carries on the tradition of Afro-American studies pioneered more than one-half century ago by W. E. B. DuBois, Guy B. Johnson, Benjamin Mays, E. Franklin Frazier and Melville Herskovits. It is, then, finally, a social anthropological contribution of the first order to the understanding of syncretic forms of religious behavior among Africans and their descendants in the New World.

1. I. 71.   William A. Shack
                                         University of California,
                                         At Berkeley

INTRODUCTION

The phenomenon of spirit possession has existed in most areas of the world down through history. The form and interpretation of the experience vary from culture to culture but there is a common substratum. Possession, to be really understood, must be studied from various points of view because no simple explanation appears adequate to explain it. It has been surprising to note that most of the authors who have written about possession have explained it from one single point of view, which could not possibly be sufficient. To understand possession it is necessary to consider the various factors involved, both singly and in conjunction with each other. These factors need not all function together in all instances, but the particular factors involved determine the character of the manifestation.

My aim in this book is to consider the various elements involved in possession, such as neurophysiology, hypnosis, socialization, and cultural determinism, to see how each one functions and what its role is alone and in relationship to the others. It is first necessary to deal with the general and fundamental features that are the underlying common substrata to be found in most possession phenomena in different social and cultural contexts. I am concerned with what possession is on various levels, from physiological to cultural, and what general role it plays in societies and in individuals. Once this general base is clarified and the mechanisms of possession understood, one may go on to study in depth particular instances of possession and their roles and functions in specific societal contexts.

Possession phenomena have been quite misunderstood in the past because the researchers did not examine their neurophysiological and hypnotic infrastructures. It is largely for this reason that people who were involved in this seemingly bizarre behavior were considered hysterical, neurotic, or psychotic. The chapters on neurophysiology and hypnosis in particular emphasize the fact that possession-like states can be brought about in perfectly normal people by various means. The authors who have judged possession abnormal have done so in general because of the similarity of its behavioral manifestations to Western pathological symptoms. Those who have said it is normal have not given any scientific basis for such assertions. They have only said it is normal because of its element of cultural determinism and because the people who get possessed seem normal to them on other occasions; but, of course, cultural determinism is also involved in pathological behavior. If it is normal it must be able to be, and can be, provoked in normal people by various processes, as the two subsequent chapters will indicate.

I think it is important to establish that possession may be a very normal culturally determined phenomenon, although some instances of possession may be manifestations of pathology, but even then of controlled pathology, in order to properly situate it and understand its role and function in a given society. In some societies or segments thereof, possession seems to be extremely highly motivated and involved role playing, whereas in others it may be a refuge for people who are really disturbed and who learn to control their disturbance through participation in a possession cult which is actually an institutionalized way of coping with such problems in the society.

In this book I am principally concerned with traditional societies in which there is communal ceremonial possession of individuals by specific deities or spirits who impart their particular personalities and behavior to the individuals possessed. I shall not consider situations in which individuals are possessed because they are or are to become diviners or mediums, or those like the Taita, in Kenya, in which individuals become possessed when they are upset, unless such situations are found in societies with ceremonial possession cults. Similar mechanisms may be involved, as is evidenced by spontaneous, non-ceremonial possession in areas with possession cults, but the social and cultural factors are different. In the groups in question the possessing deities, who are to be controlled not exorcised as is sometimes the case, come to fraternize with and help people. Therefore their manifestations are positively valued and beneficial to the individuals involved and to the community as a whole.

The principal areas of concentration are the traditional Candomblé in Bahia, Brazil, Haitian and Dahomean Vodun, the Songhay tribe of Niger, the Zar cult of Gondar, Ethiopia, the Winti cult in Dutch Guiana, and the Shango cult in Trinidad. Emphasis will also be placed on the changes such traditional cults have undergone as a result of changes in social conditions. These cults are all African or of African origin, and there have been geographical links between those on the African continent. The Yoruba of Nigeria and the Fon of Dahomey are neighbors and historically waged war against each other. As a consequence of this contact, and because their religions were originally similar in structure, their pantheons and the styles of worship of their deities are about the same, although the names of the gods are different. The possession cults in Bahia, Trinidad, and Cuba are of mainly Yoruba origin, that of Haiti principally Dahomean, and that of Dutch Guiana, largely Ghanaian. The Songhay cult was influenced by the Yoruba (the thunder god Dongo is the Yoruba Shango), and their oral tradition reports that a new family of spirits was brought from the Red Sea area, locus of the Zar cult, in the 1920's. Hence there is some geographical relationship and cultural borrowing between all of these groups. The information on Bali is included for comparative and contrastive reasons.

At this point it would be wise to consider what is meant by 'possession'. The terms 'possession' and 'trance' are often used interchangeably, but there is a difference. Trance is the scientific description of a psychological and physiological state in Western terminology, whereas possession is the folk explanation, in more philosophical terms, for the same type of state. Possession is "any native theory which explains any event of human behavior as being the result of the physical presence in a human body of an alien spirit which takes control of the host's executive functions, most frequently speech and control of the skeletal musculature" (Wallace 1959: 59). Beattie stresses the individual's state of dissociation or auto-hypnosis, or claim to illness, and the society's explanation of what it recognizes as unusual behavior as due to the control of an outside agent who either inspires the individual to act in a particular manner, or displaces the individual's personality and acts in its stead (1964: 229).

Given this distinction, trance can exist without being explained as possession, but in the societies being considered some degree of trance usually does exist, barring faking, when the term possession is used, and most states of trance and altered states of consciousness are explained as possession. Even some pathological altered states of consciousness, recognized as insanity by the society in question, are looked upon as possession by demons or spirits which are in some way evil or harmful.

Possession in folk theory is the explanation, according to Wallace, for three classes of psychosomatic behavior (1959: 59-60):

1. Obsessive ideation and compulsive action.
2. Hysterical dissociation including multiple personalities, fugues, somnambulism, and conversion hysteria.
3. Hallucinations—which he defines as "pseudoperception, without relevant stimulation of external or internal sensory receptors, but with subjective vividness equal to (or greater than) that aroused by such stimulation".

Any one or combination of the above phenomena is explicable by the mechanism of possession. Of course in terms of a given culture what Wallace describes as pseudoperception is correct perception of the culturally constituted reality. Also there is stimulation of both internal and external receptors. The external ceremonial cues provoke internal reactions and the behavior of the deity results.

Possession and hallucinations can be provoked by various means, such as drugs, sensory deprivation, physiological stress, or hypnosis or auto-hypnosis. Many societies lend little special significance to the actual concrete agent provocateur of the possession or hallucination since they as well as dreams are, in terms of folk theory, caused by the same mechanism, usually the displacement of a soul. It is the fact of possession per se which is important in that it indicates communication with the supernatural. The communication may be considered good or bad depending upon the nature of the possessing agent and the content of the possession, and these factors determine the response of the individual and of the community. Francis Huxley gave LSD to a Haitian mambo (priestess) and although her experience had been induced by a drug rather than by the normal method, her visions were particularly vivid, and she prophesied fluently in what appeared analogous to an especially good instance of possession (1966: 112-116).

The trance state must be viewed in terms of individual, interpersonal, and socio-cultural variables and situational demands. The form, purpose, and limits of the trance state can be understood only by considering the individual and his psychic structure in a given situational and cultural context. The analysis of trance states rests, according to van der Walde, on two basic assumptions. The first is that "trance states are a class of ego mechanisms designed to allow for the discharge of basic drives in a goal-oriented manner". The second, which refers to the cross-cultural comparison of trance states, is that certain basic drives indigenous to Western culture are universal and it is only in the manner of expression or discharge of these drives that cultural determinants intervene. The subject's manifestation depends upon what his culture defines as normal or abnormal, tolerates, approves, or discourages (van der Walde 1968: 57-59). The efficacy of such occasional periodic releases of suppressed impulses in reducing tensions and anxieties is widely recognized. Most cultures provide for some sort of recreative catharsis on a periodic basis, encouraging individuals on these occasions to act out wishes whose realization would be undesirable on other occasions (Wallace 1966: 190). Ritual possession in the societies under consideration provides such periodic release in allowing people to act out suppressed facets of themselves in a culturally approved and valuable manner.

According to Pierre Mabille (in Maximilien 1945) religion serves three major functions. It is a particular way of linking man with the natural and supernatural forces which surround him and which impose their power on his weakness. This supposes that man creates for himself representations of the great unknown forces, which he names and classifies, and to which he attributes certain forms; in other words he creates a coherent system of cosmogonic interpretation. Secondly, it is a mode of liaison of men among themselves. It is a social phenomenon that solidifies the human collectivity by means of public ceremonies. Religion engenders a separation between the sacred and the profane. Knowledge of and the ability to deal with the sacred becomes the domain of a particular group, some members of which are community leaders. Religion is, thirdly, a way of linking the contradictory tendencies of the individual's inner being. The individual's theater of intimate conflicts is continuously renewed, but religion, in proposing prototypes, provides a path to personal morality and helps man to overcome the anguishes that may be the product of such conflicts. This guiding path is the individual's attempt to approach the image presented to him as ideal (Maximilien 1945: xiii-xiv).

In the religions in question man understands, participates in, and to some extent dominates the natural and supernatural forces that surround him in being possessed by the deities who represent and control these forces. These deities are very human and personify the qualities considered ideal by the community. Men are linked among themselves in various ways. They must co-operate in the rituals to bring on the presence of the gods and when the gods come, the men incarnating them interact and dialogue with each other within the sacred frame of reference created by the ritual. Also people who are devotees of the same deities are felt to share common characteristics since the men are seen as reflecting the lives of the gods. The structure of the social interaction of the deities is said to determine that of the men. The contradictions within individual beings are resolved by being expressed during possession when the devotee assumes the personality of the deity or deities who manifest the normally unseen facets of himself.

In each religion, dialogue with the gods calls for specific corporeal techniques. Much Christian worship is characterized by humility, effacement, and the silence of the body. The activity of the body is suspended in conformity to the dualistic metaphysic which separates mind and body and condemns the body to effacement as the mind communes with God. Any disorganization of the senses in communication with the sacred is of diabolical origin. Mystics, communicating with God in an unorthodox manner, are considered aberrant. The Christian bodily techniques are opposed point for point to those of the possession cults of the African and Afro-American groups in question (de Heusch 1962: 128). The fundamental character of possession is the total participation of the devotees. They are not just spiritually uplifted as in Christianity, but their entire beings are put into motion. The sacred rhythms of the drums reach the depths of their beings and make them the playthings of the gods who possess them (Mabille in Maximilien 1945: xx). The African gods only live in the measure to which they are reincarnated in the flesh of their devotees, so the actual rite of possession is the supreme and most dramatic moment of the religious ceremony, when the ritual becomes a living, sacred mythology (Bastide 1958: 15).

Most of the devotees of the traditional possession cults are women, and members of the lower class or caste where there are such social distinctions. The men who are possessed are often abnormal, like the homosexuals in the Bahian Candomblé. Except in the traditional Yoruba cults in Bahia, where the Candomblé leaders are usually women, frequently past menopause, because serving and being possessed by the gods is a woman's duty, most priests are males. While women are concerned with the inner workings of the Candomblé, men are involved with its relation to the larger community. Men financially support the religious community, act as drummers, collect herbs and animals for the sacrifice which they perform. They may dance alone and soberly, but not become 'tonto' or carried away, possession being detrimental to their masculinity. Women are gods while in the temple whereas men are profane from their dealings in trade and with other women.

In Haiti there are priestesses but it seems that the priests are more important, and the literature on the other areas does not mention priestesses, except that there are priestesses in the Zar cult, but again the most important healers are men. Some groups in Brazil, which are of non-Yoruba origin or which have Indian influences, such as the Angola and Congo cults and the Catimbó, allow both men and women to be possessed, the number of women still being predominant. Among the Songhay, possession by the traditional Holey is mainly the domain of women, whereas possession by the later introduced family of Haouka concerns mainly men (Bastide 1960: 272, 402; Herskovits 1956: 160; Landes 1947: 37-38; Rouch 1960).

It is reasonable to expect women to be more prone than men to possession in most societies because their life possibilities offer them little opportunity to gain self-esteem through personal achievement, and they have less range and degree of expression of various usually suppressed drives. In caste or class societies such as the Songhay and the Zar, plus the Afro-American cults in their present settings, most of the people who become possessed, being economically and socially disadvantaged, have a great need to escape reality and become gods for a little while. In Bali, in contrast with the other areas, both men and women of all castes are trance mediums, doctors, and dancers, the only sexual distinction being that the child trance dancers are girls. It would seem that this difference is a result of the fact that the Balinese socialization process creates basic personality characteristics in everyone which are conducive to trance states, without putting particular social strains on either sex, whereas in the other areas the different male-female proportions result from the specific social and psychological pressures put on each sex and the society's expectations from them.

There are various estimates of the number of people possessed in ceremonies, which, of course, varies from area to area. Jean Rouch estimates the average Songhay proportion at about six per cent of the members of a village (1960: 188). Simpson found that in 1934 in a Haitian rural population of thirty thousand there were two hundred houngans (priests), fifteen hundred to two thousand assistants to the houngans, three thousand people who were possessed in ceremonies, and fifteen to twenty thousand members of the rank and file, believers to various degrees, who did not get possessed, which means that at least ten per cent of the population got possessed. He also says that in Northern Haiti he saw ten to twenty per cent of the ceremonial participants possessed, and that some people report having been at ceremonies where everyone was possessed, though he does not mention how many people were present or what type of ceremony it was (1945: 47). The absence of possessions in a Vodun ceremony means that the gods are angry, and the houngan must insist to make them come (Mars 1966: 24).

In traditional Nigeria and Dahomey each deity had his own cult with his own priests, societies of devotees, cult centers, and regulations. The devotees of one god could never worship any other. In the New World, however, there were not usually enough people from a particular tribe together to recreate such specialization, plus the slavery situation was hardly propitious to maintaining such formally structured organization. Also since slaves from various ethnic groups were put together rather haphazardly, their religions tended to become syncretized and all of the gods were worshipped within the same cult.

Nigerian and Dahomean cults, in their traditional state, were the most formally structured and well-regulated. The devotee had to wear special beads, the seat of the deity, without which he would not possess his devotee. The god would come only on his own worship day, in front of his cult house, to the sound of his drum rhythm, after vévés (special designs) and the proper sacrifices had been made (Herskovits 1933: 45). The devotees were isolated and initiated for a period of years. Their possessing deities were chosen for social reasons rather than to correspond to any unexpressed facets of their personalities. Thus the god personality manifest by the devotee was a learned role imposed from without, rather than a fusion between the god personality and that of the individual.

The traditional Candomblé is quite highly structured, with a relatively intact mythology. Devotees are initiated to assume the personality of the one deity they serve, but care is taken to see that the deity's personality conforms to that of the devotee. In Haiti and non-traditional Brazilian cults people may be possessed by more than one deity, expressing different facets of their personalities, and with community control breaking down as a result of social change, people are inventing private deities or beings to conform to their own personal needs rather than to any cultural dictates. Thus there is a progression from more to less structure, and from much cultural determinism and control to great individual freedom, to the detriment of both the religion as a social institution and to the mental health of the people involved.

To conclude, in this study I plan to present, synthesize, and critically examine the existing explanations and theories about ceremonial possession in the areas designated. I am synthesizing this information in order to try to understand what the phenomenon of possession is from various points of view, how it is provoked, what role it plays, and what kinds of functions it has for individuals and for societies. Only through such a synthesis is it possible to be aware of what is known and what is not, and which explanations are reasonable and which are not, and to organize this knowledge to arrive at some general conclusions leading to an awareness of the kinds of directions which should be taken in future research.

CHAPTER ONE

THE NEUROPHYSIOLOGY OF POSSESSION

The feature that is most obvious to the observer of possession phenomena is that the possessed person exhibits motor behavior very different from that which is characteristic for him. In Western psychological terms the individual may be considered to be suffering from some form of psychopathology, whereas in folk terms, a god, spirit, or demon has assumed control of his faculties. Only recently, however, has there been any special consideration of the purely neurophysiological changes experienced by the possessed individual.

It is particularly important to study the neurophysiological aspects of possession since this is obviously the common base for the individual and cultural variations of the same phenomenon. Also it is apparent that if the basis, or partial basis, of possession is found in neurophysiological changes usually resulting from external stimuli, and more rarely from psychological peculiarities, then possession should be seen as a normal, human phenomenon which may be provoked by various external means in a wide variety of types of people. Each culture imposes a specific content and significance on this common base.

Sargant (1957) uses a Pavlovian model to explain phenomena such as brainwashing and intense revivalistic-type religious experiences, which involve mechanisms similar to those involved in possession. His theory of transmarginal stimulation and inhibition interprets such phenomena as responses of the central nervous system to degrees of stimulation or deprivation of stimulation in excess of that with which the body is prepared to cope. This excess stimulation or deprivation upsets the organism to such a degree that hysteria, collapse, and/or a total disruption of previous conditioning may result. Fatigue, drugs, glandular changes, and other forms of stimulation can help lower the subject's resistence to such a breakdown. The temperament of the individual and the degree of stimulation play a large role in determining the actual form of the response obtained.

In religious and political brainwashing and conversion this mechanism is employed to condition the individual with new beliefs and behavioral patterns. Further along I will discuss the relationship of this process to the initiation period in possession cults. Of course this transmarginal stimulation and inhibition can also result in psychopathology, particularly if this is the intent. However, in possession the excess stimulation of the ceremonial situation provokes behavior beneficial to both the individual and the community.

Possession falls clearly within the category to which Ludwig refers as 'altered states of consciousness', in which he includes day dreams, sleep and dream states, hypnosis, sensory deprivation, hysterical states of dissociation and depersonalization, and pharmacologically in-duced mental aberrations (1966: 68). The effects of photic and sonic driving, the latter of which has a very obvious relationship to drum induced possession in many African and Afro-American religions, are of the same class of experience.

Altered states of consciousness are "those mental states, induced by various physiological, psychological, or pharmaceutical maneuvers, or agents, which can be recognized subjectively by the individual himself [or by an objective observer of the individual] as representing a sufficient deviation, in terms of psychological experience or psychological functioning, from certain general norms as determined by the subjective experience or psychological functioning during alert, waking consciousness. This sufficient deviation may be represented by a greater preoccupation with internal sensations or mental processes than is usual, by changes in the formal characteristics of thought, and by the impairment of reality-testing to various degrees ... ASC's may be produced in any setting by any agents or maneuvers which interfere with the normal inflow of sensory or prioceptive stimuli, and normal outflow of motor impulses, and normal 'emotional tone', or the normal flow and organization of recognitive processes" (Ludwig 1968: 69-70).

According to Ludwig, there is an optimal range of exteroceptive stimulation which is necessary to maintain normal waking consciousness, including normal perceptual, motor, emotional, and cognitive experience. Levels above and below this range are conducive to the production of ASC's (1968: 70). This correlates with Sargant's transmarginal stimulation and inhibition theory.

Ludwig distinguishes five types of situations which usually result in ASC's (1968: 71-75):

1. Reduction of exteroceptive stimulation and/or motor activity
   —result of absolute reduction of sensory input, changes in pattern of

sensory data, or constant exposure to repetitive, monotonous stimuli.
—includes hypnotic trance; ASC's from prolonged social isolation, e.g., mystics, aescetics.
—[lethargy of initiation period].
2. Increase of exteroceptive stimulation and/or motor activity and/or emotion
—excitatory mental states resulting mainly from sensory overloading or bombardment, which may or may not be accompanied by strenuous physical activity or exertion. Profound emotional arousal and mental fatigue may be major contributing factors.
—dance and music trance in response to rhythmic drumming; hyperkinetic trance states associated with emotional mental contagion, often in group or mob setting; religious conversion and healing trance experiences during revivalistic meetings; mental aberrations associated with certain rites of passage; spirit possession states; shamanistic, divinatory, prophetic and ecstatic trances.
3. Increased alertness or mental involvement
—results from focused or selective hyperalertness and result of peripheral hyperalertness for prolonged periods.
—fervent praying; total involvement in listening to dynamic speaker; trance resulting from watching a revolving object.
4. Decreased alertness or relaxation of critical faculties
—passive state of mind with minimum of active, goal-directed thinking.
5. Presence of somatopsychological factors
—results from alterations in body chemistry or neurophysiology which are deliberate or because of a situation over which the individual has no control.
—drowsiness; dehydration; hypoglycemia from fasting; [hyperventilation]; hormone disturbance; sleep deprivation.

The same basic process, transmarginal stimulation or inhibition, is operative to varying degrees in all of Ludwig's categories. He notes that some ASC's can be used to facilitate the emergence of others as well as to eliminate, control, structure, or direct them (1968: 85).

It is most important to note that in possession more than one of the above factors is usually involved. The specific factors involved and their manner and degree of involvement determine the character of the particular possession. Different factors seem to be operative in different societies as well as in different types of possession within the same society, and even in the same individual on different ceremonial and non-ceremonial occasions. The initial stages of possession may be due to one factor and later states to another. For example, in many instances the onset of possession is a violent response to the bombardment of excessive sensory stimulation. The following phase, the settling of the god, may then be characterized by very deliberate comportment conforming to the personality of the god, which is evidence of increased emotional and mental concentration on and involvement in the mythological system.

Ludwig cites a number of characteristic features of altered states of consciousness (1968: 77-83):

1. Alteration in thinking
   —inward shift in direction of attention; disturbed memory, concentration, judgement.
2. Disturbed time sense.
3. Loss of control
   —may gain greater control or truth through loss of conscious control, e.g., identity with source of greater power.
4. Change in emotional expression
   —less control, inhibition; more primitive, extreme emotions; may be detached.
5. Body image changes
   —depersonalization, body-mind schism, dissolution of boundaries between self and others or universe, feeling of oneness or transcendence.
6. Perceptual distortions — hallucinations and pseudohallucinations
   —content of perceptual aberrations determined by culture, group, individual, [and]/or neurophysiological factors. May represent wish fulfillment, expression of basic fears or conflicts, or phenomena of little dynamic importance.
7. Change in meaning or significance
   —attach increased meaning or significance to subjective experiences, ideas, perceptions in such state; often feelings of profound truth, insight, illumination. This feeling of increased significance or importance is one of most important features of religious or mystical consciousness, and is probably a major feature in stabilizing many religious groups.
8. Sense of ineffable
   —because unique, subjective experience, hard to communicate nature or essence to one who has not undergone it; tendency not to remember.
9. Feelings of rejuvenation, renewed hope.
10. Hypersuggestibility
    —increased propensity of person to accept and/or automatically respond to specific statements, i.e., commands or instructions of leader, or to non-specific cues as cultural group expectations. The distinguishing feature of these states is the hypnotized subject's emotional conviction that the world is as suggested by the hypnotist rather than a pseudo-perception based on this suggestion. There is also a reduction of the effective range of the

critical faculties with an attendant decrease in the capacity for reality testing, i.e., an inability to distinguish between subjective and objective reality. This situation creates a compensatory need to bolster such faculties by seeking props and guidance in an effort to relieve the anxiety usually associated with such a loss of control. There is increased reliance on an authority who is seen as omnipotent.

With the 'dissolution of self boundaries', an important feature of ASC's, the subject has a tendency to identify with an authority [in possession this would be the god or spirit, priest, and total community] whose wishes and commands are seen as the individual's own. As a result of all these factors there occurs a monomotivational or supramotivational state in which the person strives to realize in concrete behavior, the thoughts or ideas he experiences as subjective reality. This subjective reality is determined by the expectations of the authority figure or group as well as by the individual's own wishes and fears. In an altered state of consciousness in which external direction and structure are ambiguous or ill-defined (e.g., panic, acute psychosis) the person's internal mental productions are his major guide in the perception of reality, and thus have a large role in determining his behavior. In this case the subject is more susceptible to the dictates of his emotions and the fantasies and thoughts associated with them than to the directions given by other people.

Ludwig emphasizes the fact that although similar basic processes may operate in the production of different ASC's, such influences as cultural expectations, demand characteristics, communications factors, transference feelings, personal motivations and expectancies (mental set), and the specific processes used to induce the ASC work together to shape the resultant mental state with its own unique flavor (1968: 75).

Prince would classify possession as one of a wider class of psychomotor amnesic states, which includes psychomotor epilepsy, sleepwalking, hypnotically induced somnambulistic states, and some forms of multiple personalities. These states are all characterized by (1968: 121):

1. Altered states of consciousness.
2. Elaborate motor behavior.
3. Subsequent amnesia for the duration of the altered state of consciousness.

Some psychomotor amnesic states are associated with gross neurophysiological changes which show up in electroencephalograms. The EEG of a sleepwalker is different from that of the waking state, but there are no EEG changes, according to Prince, in hysterical trance states, fits, or other dissociative phenomena, or in hypnotically induced trance states. In some ways possession is like a hysterical fugue state or hypnotically induced trance. However, several features of possession are unlike features of these phenomena, and do suggest basic neurophysiological alterations (Prince 1968: 125-127).

The following features are usually associated with possession (Prince 1968: 127-129):

1. Induction of possession state frequently achieved by dancing to music with a pronounced and rapid beat.
2. It frequently follows a period of starvation and/or overbreathing
   —hypoglycemia and overbreathing both cause a slowing of the brain waves, as little as three minutes of the latter being sufficient to effect the change.
3. Onset of possession period marked by brief period of inhibition or collapse.
4. In neophytes collapse may be followed by period of hyperactivity; once experience is acquired, controlled, deity-specific behavior pattern emerges.
5. During state of possession frequent fine tremors of head and limbs and sometimes grosser, convulsive jerks; diminution of sensory acuity may be evident
   —the initial collapse state, muscular jerks, and fine tremors suggest neurophysiological changes.
6. Return to normal consciousness followed by sleep of exhaustion from which subject awakens in state of mild euphoria.

One of the most obvious features in the production of ceremonial possession, which is not present in the other psychomotor amnesic states, is rhythmic stimulation, usually drumming, but also chanting, and in Bali actual shaking of the child trance dancers.[1] Observation of the frequent use of drumming to produce possession led Neher (1962) to do laboratory experiments on human responses to sonic driving, following the principle of photic driving. In photic driving a bright light flashes at a frequency near that of the basic (alpha)

---

[1] The little girls as well as the trance mediums are also smoked with incense. One effect of this smoking is probably hyperventilation. It is also possible that the incense itself may have some effect. Bowers notes that a black powder was pounded to create a fog-like dust during a Haitian ceremony which she attended. She did not find out what the dust was, but it acted as an irritant and stimulant. She found herself very alert after having fought against drowsiness until that point. The dancers coughed and sneezed after they finished dancing, but not while they danced, although that was when most of the dust was in the air. There were more possessions during this dance than during others she observed (1961: 275).

rhythm of the brain waves. Two electrical effects result. The brain waves increase in amplitude and if the frequency of the light source is shifted somewhat, the brain waves adjust to the new frequency. The behavioral effects of both photic and sonic driving are visual hallucinations, kinesthetic sensations, alterations in feeling state, e.g., fear, anger, pleasure, confusion, and in some cases psychopathic states, and myoclonic jerks at the frequency of the stimulus or one of its subharmonics. Also in people suffering from a neurophysiological disturbance, a full scale grand mal seizure may occur (Neher 1962: 153-154; Walter and Grey 1949: 65). Rhythmic stimulation often evokes responses both quantitatively and qualitatively different from those associated with steady excitation of the same receptors because these rhythmic signals seem to reach parts of the central nervous system inaccessible to non-rhythmic stimuli, however intense (Walter and Grey 1949: 81).

The most dramatic results are seen in people with personal or family histories of neurophysiological disturbances, and no generalized seizures were observed in subjects without this type of background. Many of the sensations experienced by the normal subject would be considered abnormal in the absence of photic or sonic stimulation, but unless the subject is in some way predisposed, the abnormalities usually do not spread to more than a few circuits, and usually result only in subjective sensations. These are usually vivid enough to evoke appropriate somatic responses, e.g., righting reflexes in those with kinesthetic illusions. Anomalous effects tend to subside in normal individuals and increase in abnormal individuals after about a half hour (Walter and Grey 1949: 63, 65, 83). Hence it seems that the great majority of the people who become possessed can not be epileptics [as it is generally defined] or otherwise seriously neurophysiologically disturbed, as some have posited in the past, because if they were they could not exhibit the degree of control which they do. This is not to say that many do not probably have a genetic propensity to experience neurophysiological changes with ease, since most people who become possessed belong to families with a long history of possession.

The subjective sensations and somatic effects of photic and sonic driving vary over a wide range, correlating in part with the amplitude, frequency, and location in the brain of the evoked response. In most subjects the onset of a particularly vivid illusion or hallucination is preceded or accompanied by a characteristic alteration in electrical response. Some of the most striking changes reported occurred when the subject reinforced a sensation evoked by a stimulus with a pleasant or unpleasant image from his memory or imagination. The individual actually may exercise some conscious control. Voluntary inhibition of the illusory sensations evoked by the stimulus often attenuates the electrical response, and distracting rather than reinforcing mental activity involving visual imagery generally diminishes the intensity of the evoked responses as well as the alpha wave alterations (Walter and Grey 1949:63).

Such features account for many of the general characteristics of possession. The experience is very vivid because there is a very strong cultural pattern which provides material to reinforce and give content and meaning to the neurological responses. The resultant behavior is seen as an expression of the personal characteristics of the possessing deity. That this reinforcement may be pleasant or disagreeable corresponds to the idea that the possessed individual is acting out unconscious desires which may be unpleasant if he unconsciously wants to inflict punishment on himself for some feeling of guilt, as well as pleasant. Also the fact that one can voluntarily inhibit the changes in brain waves as well as the evoked sensations explains why some people who are susceptible do not get possessed when they do not want to or should not for some socio-cultural reason. In Haiti some people become 'drunk' (saoulé) by the gods without becoming actually possessed. This deliberate avoidance of possession is probably a result of mentally inhibiting by auto-suggestion the evocation of somatic responses and the changes in brainwave pattern. The houngans (priests) in Haiti who officiate while apparently possessed must be especially adept at controlling their states and remaining very lucid. Devotees have many gimmicks to avoid possession, such as fixing their hair in special ways or having crossed safety pins or hair pins on their person to tie down or trap the god. These gimmicks undoubtedly function by reinforcing and focusing the concentration of the devotees on their desire not to be possessed. When they are possessed despite these gimmicks it is probably because of an unconscious desire to be possessed which is stronger than the conscious desire not to be.

In laboratory experiments it was shown that a combination of additional factors reinforced the effects of simple rhythmic stimulation (Neher 1962: 153-156):

1. Rhythms accompanying the main rhythm, particularly those that are multiples [or fractions] of it, heighten the response, as does
2. Rhythmic stimulation in more than one sensory mode at a time.
3. General stress increases susceptibility to rhythmic stimulation. Overbreathing was particularly used in the laboratory, and violent ceremonial dancing may produce hyperventilation and cause a decrease in the blood glucose used for energy. Low blood glucose, as well as the production of adrenalin from over-exertion and fatigue increase susceptibility. Adrenochrome, a compound which has been isolated from adrenalin (though it has not been found in isolation in the body), is related to every hallucinogen whose composition is known.

In Haiti and Brazil there are always three drums, one, the Mama, carrying the main beat, and the others reinforcing it and improvising around it. The people are stimulated in several senses simultaneously because in addition to hearing the drums they are singing and dancing to the rhythm, and watching others do so at the same time. The dancers dance with great violence, energy, and concentration, getting really involved in the rhythm and movement. Both Métraux (1958: 139) and Ravenscroft (1965: 177) suggest that the dancers' motions simulate the behavior of the possessed state as a physical technique to achieve it. Since possession comes easily after the first few times this technique, along with the other concurrent stimuli, usually rapidly brings on the desired state.

Since many people involved in these religious groups are poor, they undoubtedly do not have well-balanced diets or even sufficient food in many cases. It has been shown in a laboratory that fasting subjects, both normal and abnormal, had more anomalous experiences than when their blood sugar was at a more normal level.

Neher suggests that the rhythmic stimulation of drumming may also have an anaesthetic effect (1962: 159). People while possessed frequently undergo such ordeals as walking on hot coals or sticking their arms in boiling oil, which would be very painful under normal conditions. Laboratory experiments have shown that strong sensory stimulation concurrent with pain can inhibit the transmission of pain signals to the conscious areas of the brain. Another explanation for the same phenomenon is hypnotic anaesthesia.

According to Neher, most individual brain wave frequencies are from eight to thirteen cycles per second. This is thus the most effective range for obtaining responses to rhythmic light stimuli. A slightly lower range for sound stimuli is more effective because of slower frequencies in the auditory region of the cortex. Hence one would expect to find most drum rhythms for possession ceremonies slightly below eight to thirteen beats per second. In Africa many dance rhythms have been found with seven to nine beats per second. In Haitian Vodun music agitated behavior occurs when drum rhythms reach eight or nine beats per second. This is neither the fastest rhythm possible nor is it particularly easy for the drummers to maintain (1962: 154).

Brain wave frequencies vary from person to person but are essentially constant in one person over time, as is the frequency at which a person is most susceptible to rhythmic stimulation. One's emotional response is greatest at the point of highest driving. Neher also expects to find that the frequency of these drum rhythms is changed often to encompass the gamut of individual frequencies present, and that particular individuals would be more susceptible to certain rhythms (1962: 155). This is, of course, true since each god has his own rhythm which brings him into the heads of his devotees.

People differ in their degree of susceptibility to rhythmic stimulation, which may be attributable to anatomical variations, age, and differences in personality (Walter and Grey 1949: 18). Genetic factors are apparently also very important. Changes in an individual's responses are produced by somatic, mental, and emotional changes, whether spontaneous and voluntary, or induced. Also, somatic, mental, and emotional changes can be induced in a subject by rhythmic stimulation at the proper frequencies, and these two effects can interact with each other. A man, for example, whose brainwave frequency was eleven cycles per second, habitually responded with disgust when the stimulus frequency was lowered to seven or eight flashes per second (Walter and Grey 1949: 79, 85).

Walter and Grey suggest that with proper psychological analysis some correlation should be found between the character of the evoked response to rhythmic stimulation and the way the subjects think, with reference to such traits as originality or creative imagination (1949: 77, 84). This idea correlates with Sarbin's point that some people have more role-taking aptitude than others (1950). Of course the problem arises as to how to define and quantify such qualities, but it seems that some type of test could be designed to do just this.

Perhaps the people who habitually become possessed in ceremonies are those who are the most creative, either those who actually are creative in everyday life or those whose creativity is stifled by either psychological or social factors. Projective tests could perhaps be revealing in this realm.

Also, each god has his own personal rhythm to which his devotees respond. Since there is in most cases some correlation between the personality of the god and that of his devotee, it would be interesting to see if there is also one between the god's personality and the rhythm which brings him into the head of his devotees, particularly since changes in the frequency of rhythmic stimulation can cause changes in affective state. In Haiti a person may be possessed by several different gods in succession, however, none of the literature says whether or not this is always in direct response to changes in drum rhythm. Since each god is supposedly called individually by the drums, with the priest as choreographer, it would seem that this should be the case. If it could be shown that the rhythm is similar for a specific type of god personality in different areas, this would indicate that there is probably a correlation.

Some people are so conditioned to their rhythms that whenever they hear them, under any kind of circumstances, they are possessed. Herskovits said that the Dahomeans would not listen to their own drum rhythm except in ceremonies because they feared that they would begin dancing and be unable to stop before they died. A Dahomean priest did eventually record his deity's rhythm for Herskovits with no problem (1938). Since he was a priest he probably had more control over his deity and could control his possessions. Herskovits also recorded an instance of a man's becoming possessed in Dutch Guiana while recording the songs of his god (1966: 297). Bastide, however, in insisting that possession is subject to social more than psychological control, states that people who are normally possessed when hearing the rhythm of their deities are not possessed if they are in certain states, such as mourning, in which one should not be possessed (1953: 45). There is obviously interaction between neurophysiological and psychological control of possession. Although a devotee begins to be possessed, it may be possible for him to exert his will against this occurrence. According to Walter and Grey, the normal brain can stop the effects of photic or sonic driving by consciously banishing phantom sensations. Even some epileptics can, by mental concentration or some other means, change conditions enough to break the chain reaction at its weakest link before rhythmic stress has gone too far. Once a certain proportion of central circuits has been drawn in, no degree of concentration, not even stopping the stimulus, can break the feedback loop (1949: 83).

Since responses to sonic and photic driving are greatest at the point of highest driving, one would expect the rhythm to increase in rapidity over the course of the ceremony, which is indeed the case, and more and more people are possessed. In the Candomblé, there is first the salute to the gods, followed by calls to individual gods to possess their devotees. The culmination is the irresistable call to all of the gods, during which many of those who have hitherto resisted possession must succumb. In shamanic ceremonies among the Tungus of Siberia, there is initially slow, soft drumming to concentrate the attention of both shaman and audience, then when contact is made with the spirit [probably through the shaman's auto-hypnosis], an assistant takes the drum and drums louder and faster to maintain the shaman's ecstasy and to control the audience. A passage from Wittkower evokes the atmosphere of the Haitian Vodun ceremony: "As the beating of the drums became louder and faster, the singing increased in intensity and assumed a screaming quality, the collective tension mounted and a state of excitement which enveloped the whole crowd developed" (1964: 74).

Walter and Grey found that if two light sources were used simultaneously, flashing at independent frequencies, the hallucinations were so compelling that subjects could sketch them weeks later (1949: 63). Analogously, in possession ceremonies, as previously stated, there are three drums, one with the basic beat and the others reinforcing it and improvising around it. When people are observed to be approaching possession, a deliberate attempt is usually made to drive them on. The priest may push the individual toward the drums, or merely concentrate attention on him. The drummers, who have a great deal of control during the ceremonies since it is they who bring the gods, can play certain signals in the rhythmic pattern to cause the dancing to take a violent turn. They have certain rhythms which cause excitement, causing people to lurch and only regain their balance just before falling. One method is for one drum to syncopate the rhythm slightly (another one maintaining it) such that a strong beat falls just before the main beat (e.g., an eight or sixteenth note before the main beat). This gives the impression of increased speed when this is not really the case, and creates tension and a feeling of imbalance in the listener or dancer. This additional accentuated beat falls just before the dancer actually puts his foot down, causing him to lurch forward in an attempt to catch the main beat, which of course he can not since there are now two heavy beats in rapid succession.

Maya Deren, an American dancer who was herself possessed on several occasions by Erzulie Dahomey, the Haitian goddess of love, gives, from personal experience, a good indication of the degree of control of the drummer of the Mama drum. He can 'break' to relieve the tension of the monotonous beat and bodily motion, thus interrupting concentration. By withholding this break he can bring the Loa into the heads of the participants or stop them from coming. He can also use the break in another way by letting the tension build to a point where the break does not release tension, but climaxes it in a galvanizing shock. This enormous blow empties the dancer's head, leaving him without a center around which to stabilize. He is buffeted by the strokes as the drummer 'beats the Loa into his head'. He cringes at the large beats, clutches for support, recapturing his balance just to be hurtled forward by another great beat on the drum. The drummer, apparently impervious to the person's anguish, persists until the violence suddenly ceases, and the person lifts his head, seeming to gaze into another world. The Loa has arrived (Deren 1953: 242).

Sometimes a drummer who has begun to concentrate on one individual on the brink of possession must return to the beat for the sake of the other dancers before this devotee's Loa is installed. The person may return to normal, but is more frequently merely abandoned by the drum in limbo between mortality and divinity. Only the houngan can help bring on the Loa by concentrating all his attention on the devotee, looking deeply into his eyes, shaking his sacred rattle, talking to the Loa in a monotonous, authoritative, esoteric language, etc. The drummers even have control over the houngan. Seeing possession threaten to overcome the houngan who must execute complex ritual functions, the Mama drummer can relieve the situation by making the drumming less intense. By maintaining the rhythm he can force the houngan to become possessed (Deren 1953: 239, 243).

One important feature which reinforces the power of the drums is that the sound of the drums is the voice of the gods—both the means of calling them and their response. Thus the sounds and the drums themselves are sacred. The gods, upon arriving, salute the drums as well as the priest, because it is the drums which have made possible their manifestation (Deren 1953: 238, 246).

There are also certain rhythms which send the gods away when they come uninvited or stay too long, and at the end of the ceremony. These are gay, very lively rhythms that break the tension of both dancers and spectators. Bowers reports that once in her city garden a drummer played a Haitian rhythm for the calling down of the gods. All of the dogs within blocks howled and everyone present felt disturbed. He then played other rhythms at the same volume. The dogs were silent and the spectators felt calm again (1961: 278).

This seems to be good evidence that some particular rhythms do have purely neurophysiological effects which, as has been seen, may interact with psychological and other factors. In ceremonies some people are seen to visibly react to the drums, trembling, holding tightly to rafters, and drinking water to avoid being possessed. Some can resist, others succumb. The houngan can help either way by the way he focuses his attention. The drums are an important factor but not totally sufficient. Their effect may be reinforced or counteracted by psychological, socio-cultural, or other physiological factors.

It would obviously be very useful to actually measure the physiological and psychological responses of participants in ceremonies. There are two ways to study the neurophysiological effects of possession. One is to induce such a state in a laboratory and study it electroencephalographically and biochemically. Of course it would be impossible to recreate all of the elements of the ceremonial situation. The other method would be to study the participants in real ceremonies. This would, of course, be more difficult, but obviously more valid. It would be necessary to use small EEG devices which would allow complete freedom of movement.

Neher poses some very significant questions which must be clarified for a real understanding of the phenomenon of possession (1962: 158-159):

1. Why do some societies and not others use drums to induce possession? The response may serve as an escape from reality, like alcohol, as a mechanism to relieve tension and inhibitions and promote group unity and feeling.
2. Is susceptibility to drum beats largely hereditary or more dependent upon acquired personality traits? Initial susceptibility to rhythmic lights seems to follow a pattern of genetic transmission.
3. Is susceptibility to drum beats in any way adaptive or maladaptive, thus subject to selection? If so do different societies show different rates of susceptibility? A study using light stimuli showed no difference between South African blacks and whites.

Question one is dealt with in other parts of this study, although I cannot say why some societies have drum-induced possession and others do not. In respect to question two it is apparent that heredity plays an important role in a person's susceptibility to neurophysiological changes resulting from rhythmic stimulation. The importance of cultural and environmental features must be emphasized. Factors such as nutrition and attitude toward such phenomena also play a very large role. If susceptibility to the type of state which may result from such stimulation is a positive value, more people will be susceptible because they will have a positive, culturally determined psychological impetus. More interdisciplinary research is necessary before a response can be given to question three, but it is first necessary to determine generally what possession is.

What has hitherto been discussed is ceremonial possession. In Haiti especially, and in some of the other areas to a lesser degree, there is also non-ceremonial possession in which an individual is possessed by his deity in a situation of extreme stress with which he can not cope. In becoming his god he is able to satisfactorily deal with the upsetting circumstances. It seems reasonable that some similar neurophysiological mechanisms are involved although the rhythmic drumming is lacking. In the areas of the world where possession-like phenomena exist outside of ceremonial occasions, they appear similar to this Haitian spontaneous possession.

Cannon's (1942) concept of 'voodoo death' accounts for people who die from an extreme stress reaction because they have broken a taboo or committed some terrible act for which there is no possible redress. The body is under such a strain in responding, over an extended period of time, to the intense fear and sense of inexorable doom felt by the individual, that death ensues quite rapidly, although the victim was previously healthy. Thus it seems reasonable that very stressful situations can also create a temporary state of transmarginal stimulation leading to the altered state of consciousness of possession for which the culture provides the mold.

According to Wallace, prolonged states of psychodynamically and socially determined stress can produce temporary changes in body chemistry. Nutritional deficiencies may contribute to such changes. As hysteria may be a symptomatic consequence of hypocalcemia, Haitian susceptibility to non-ceremonial possession may be related to some chemical result of their undernourished condition, such as hypoglycemia, in interaction with situational stress. Such chemical disturbances may result in tetany, the neurological symptoms of which involve characteristic muscular spasms of the hands, feet, throat, face, and other musculature, with major convulsive seizures in severe attacks. This tetanic syndrome, which may be precipitated by trivial circumstances, is often complicated by emotional and cognitive disorganization. Genetic factors may be responsible for the differential vulnerabilities of various members of a population to such noxious influences (Wallace 1961b: 266, 273, 288). Non-ceremonial possession, like ceremonial possession, thus appears to be a basically normal, neurophysiological reaction to some kind of stress, often combined with other contributing physiological features, the manifestation and content of which are determined by cultural factors, and thus can take various forms.

CHAPTER TWO

POSSESSION AND HYPNOSIS

The concatenation of manifestations which are part of the possession phenomenon can be explained in large part within the framework of hypnosis and hypnotically induced behavior. Therefore, most normal spirit possession may be classified as part of the gamut of hypnotoform states. Gill and Brenman consider hypnosis to be a particular kind of regressive process which may be initiated by sensory-motor-and ideational deprivation, or by the stimulation of an archaic relationship with the hypnotist. When the regressive process has been set in motion by either of these factors, phenomena characteristic of the other emerge. Their formulation links two factors which had been held singly responsible for hypnosis—altered ego functioning and transference relationships (1959: xix-xx).

The authors stress the fact that the ego can become unseated by either of these two means, although in hypnosis both are usually applied simultaneously. Also, in any particular instance of hypnotizability, the more important is the manipulation of sensory-motor and ideational deprivation, the less important is the transference relationship. Changes in ego organization and functioning initiated by such deprivation may result in any one of a number of states related to hypnosis: brown study, pre-sleep state, trance-like self-absorption as in yoga, burst of creativity, etc. Each state is characterized by a particular ego organization, and has a special 'something more' than the unseating of the ego that distinguishes it from the others (1959: xx, 30-31, 197).

Gill and Brenman classify the ego functions as (1959: 44):

1. Self-awareness.
2. Acting to tone down intensive drives, which are usually instinctual in nature.
3. Delaying gratification of impulses and/or postponing their motor expression.
4. Processes of perception and thought [The Haitians see these processes as the province of the 'gros-bon-ange', one of man's souls which is replaced by a Loa in possession].

All of these functions are disturbed in both hypnosis and possession.

The possessed person's self-awareness is obviously different since he thinks and acts as if he has become a deity. In behaving as the deity he may gratify his impulses, even when socially unacceptable, without being held responsible for his behavior. Since his whole frame of reference is different, his perceptions and thoughts must be in accord with his new state. Gill and Brenman distinguish between hysteria and hypnosis, with which I would class ceremonial possession, by the fact that in hysteria the subject transforms his own fantasies into reality and fulfills his own wishes, whereas in hypnosis it is the subject's relation to the hypnotist, rather than the former's own underlying impulses, which dominates the situation. The hypnotisand-hypnotist relationship is the 'something more' which distinguishes hypnosis and possession from related states (1959: 71). This essential factor is the element of cultural determinism which gives possession its unique character and function for the individual and the society in which it is found.

Gill and Brenman would thus define hypnosis as a situation in which one person is temporarily and within definite limits controlled by another in a setting of an initial altered state of ego functioning. The something more needed is a relationship of an archaic kind, (based largely on unconsious motivation) to another person. The induction process, of necessity, involves maximum attention and this specific kind of relationship (1959: 30-31). An analogous situation obtains in possession except that the hypnotist is not just a person.

The drumming, dancing, and singing of the religious ceremony stimulate an altered state of consciousness or altered state of ego functioning. There are several objects of transference. In many instances the priest acts specifically as a hypnotist, directing both the possessed people and their possessing deities. He determines when each deity will be called and sent away. He may, to some extent, control the intensity of an individual's possession, calming him or making him more violent, if the deity is mistreating an undeserving devotee or not being harsh enough with one who should be punished. He will also send a deity away if the devotee's physical constitution can not bear the hyperactivity of the possession state. If someone is approaching possession the priest may devote his full attention to him, staring intently into his eyes, and talking to him in an insistent monotone, perhaps in an esoteric language, commanding the deity to come, to establish a new equilibrium in the devotee on a sacred rather than profane level, and bringing him out of the limbo between the mortal and divine states. The priest is seen by the participants as having absolute authority because he mediates between them and the gods. He must thus be sensitive to and respond capably to individual needs.

The whole community is, in an important sense, the object of transference because the individual can feel free to abandon himself with no fear of harm, either physical or social. He will be taken care of by the spectators or attendants, so he may become totally dependent. In Bahia, when he becomes possessed he will be taken by attendants into a sanctuary and dressed in the costume of his god, in which he will dance. In Haiti, care will be taken to see that he does not tear his clothes or hurt himself or any spectators.

The deities who people the religious pantheon of the community are the most essential elements in the multifactor role of hypnotist. The personalities of the deities provide the suggestions which determine the behavior of the possessed people. Each deity has a distinct character and the behavior of his devotees is determined accordingly. No direct suggestions need be made by the priest or spectators because since all members of the society have from childhood seen the deities manifest themselves in people, they are familiar with the behavior pattern of each deity. The suggestion of a person's own deity's behavior has been inculcated during his lifetime religious training, and may be more deliberately and profoundly impressed upon him during an initiation period. Hence, when the possession state is induced, the individual already knows exactly how to behave according to the collective belief system of his community.

The deity is also the principle object of transference of responsibility for the devotee's behavior when possessed. The deity has taken control of the devotee's executive faculties, hence he alone is responsible for what the possessed person does. The latter, while possessed, can fulfill conscious and unconscious desires and impulses and act out fantasies forbidden under normal circumstances, but only the deity is considered responsible, and the deity's behavior can, of course, not be questioned by mere mortals. Thus, in the terms of Gill and Brenman, the hypnotist, in this case the deity, is incorporated to replace the superego and ego functions which have been relinquished to him (1959: 86-87). In native terms the deity comes into the head of his devotee, or the deity as rider mounts the devotee who is his horse.

In hypnosis as in possession the first step is usually to detach the subject from his normal external and internal realities in order to create new ones for him. Maximilien stresses the need for the devotee to lose his sense of self and to feel depersonalized and at one with the community in bringing on the deity. The subject must lose his sense of individualism to merge with the whole community in a relationship of reciprocal service and fulfillment (1945: 85-86). Much emphasis is placed on deranging the subject's sensory-motor and ideational processes. The maintenance of a normal sense of reality depends in part upon a steady flow of cues from outside, which are constantly organized by the individual with the help of internal stimuli. The aim in sensory-motor and ideational deprivation is thus to interfere with normal stimuli, and in breaking the subject's moorings with reality, alter his bodily awareness, one of the most important sources of the sense of self. The hypnotist can then convince the subject that he is losing control of himself, and that this control is being responsibly taken over by the hypnotist. The hypnotist tries to take control of as many as possible of the functions normally held by the subject's senses, bodily control, and initiating and judging mechanisms. In return, the subject is to have a rewarding experience, which also fulfills the universal infantile need for such wholesale abdication. The good hypnotic subject is characterized by an extreme eagerness to do the bidding of the hypnotist (Gill and Brenman 1959: 6-11).

The altered body image in itself creates the illusion of alterations in the setting and the individual's own identity, external and internal reality. Sonic driving alone can produce this kind of change in awareness. The hypnotist can create an entirely new reality for the subject in which the customary rules of behavior do not hold, and superego condemnation for the gratification of unacceptable wishes is not applicable, thus there is no guilt or inhibition (van der Walde 1968: 63-64). In possession, the participant's self-awareness is shaken by the neurophysiological effect of the constant rhythms. The familiar, stereotyped dancing associated with each god's rhythm causes the subject to focus all his attention on the god. Everyone knows when each god is to arrive so that the attention of all present is focused on a mental image of him. The people to be possessed by him become completely mentally and physically involved with the image and idea of the deity, who brings with him his own reality for the possessed individuals (Ravenscroft 1965: 171, 176-177).

Possession, like hypnosis, is characterized by an induction period consisting of different dynamics from the fixed state, and in both phenomena the induction period lessens in duration and degree as the individual becomes more experienced. Both may be characterized by physical and mental disequilibrium, intense outbursts of affect, violent activity, dizziness, trembling, and sometimes spasms and convulsions (Gill and Brenman 1959: 12-20; Ravenscroft 1965: 172). Once the hypnotic state or the presence of the god is established, behavior is once again calm. Calmness in possession refers to a suitable habituation of the devotee to the behavior of the possessing deity, which is not always calm in the ordinary sense of the term. The ego functions are now reorganized according to a new principle after a brief disorganization.

In considering possession, a question arises as to the degree to which the possessed person has actually become detached from reality in taking on the personality of the god. Some people appear quite lucid at times, as if their possession were just an act, yet at other times they appear to be in a deep trance. When the presiding priest is possessed, as is frequent in Haiti, he seems usually to be quite conscious and in control of the situation, as is, according to Dr. Bowers, herself a hypnotist, often noted in experienced hypnotists who, for similar reasons, have trained themselves never to indulge in the complete relaxation of deep trance (1961: 277). These priests can rely on their vast knowledge and intuitive talents to diagnose and treat illnesses while possessed, and can go into possession very easily because of their familiarity with the state (Kiev 1961b: 134).

Child trance dancers in Bali report being unconscious when they are being put into and taken out of their trances but conscious during the period of dancing (Bateson and Mead 1942: 92). It is evident that the possessed people are somewhat conscious of their real environment in ceremonial situations because they react to it. They will, for example, talk to spectators about features of their lives.

Members of the Zar cult are not totally unconscious during or amnesic after their possessions because they can describe how possession feels different from their normal state. Some people speak of the Zar in the first rather than third person, recognizing that there is not the total separation between the individual and his deity which supposedly exists in the other groups in question. Some Zar cult members can describe their gradual loss of consciousness and the take-over of their faculties by the Zar. Long-time devotees imply that there is a struggle for control between the individual and the Zar.

When the devotee cedes to his deity it is a choice he makes based on his expectation of the behavior he will exhibit (Leiris 1958: 84-85).

Belo suggests two possible reasons for which experienced trancers seem to be quite in touch with reality rather than really carried away by their experience. Trancers and normally possessed devotees become accustomed, from long practice, to entering such a state as a result of only slight dissociation because of their familiarity with the trance role. They can behave as if they are deeply entranced while maintaining contact with reality. They may, on the other hand, be in a very deep trance, but because of long practice they are no longer as concerned with the strangeness of the sensations experienced as is the less experienced person. Hence the experienced individual can be less introverted in his view of his state and give more attention to events outside himself. Younger trancers appear more absorbed in their trances than older ones (1960: 140-141). This is commensurate with the fact that older devotees and priests in Bahia and Haiti feel that they control their deities rather than being subservient to them. Also the fact that initial possessions tend to be violent and subsequent ones less so is probably related to the fact that there are more emotions to be released in the first manifestations than in the later ones which may be anticipated at regular intervals. Also, as the devotee becomes more experienced and accustomed to his state he can better control himself in general.

Gill and Brenman note that hypnotic subjects report frequent spontaneous changes in their depth of hypnosis. These are related to the psychological and emotional climate of the moment. Such changes are often accompanied by anxiety and indicate that the impulse-defense balance is being threatened by an upsurge of hostility or increased dependency needs or new cues from the external environment. The subject deals with such threats by a shift in the depth of hypnosis in an attempt to gratify or defend against new impulses which arise. The same subject may deal with the accompanying anxiety by sometimes going deeper into trance and sometimes disrupting it. The complex and subtle changes in ego functioning in hypnosis are caused by a continuous fluctuation of the organization of the ego in response to different situational demands. Hypnosis significantly alters the defense mechanism of repression but it is not known if it affects other defenses (1959: 34). This explanation perhaps accounts for the observed apparent changes in depth of possession. To be more certain, it would be necessary to observe the external circumstances surrounding such changes in depth, as well as any hints from the individual as to the changes taking place within him.

Possession sometimes ends spontaneously because of some personal experience or motivational change on the part of the possessed person without any apparent external counterpart. It more frequently ends as a result of specific changes in the external social reality. The usual cause is that the ceremonial emphasis shifts from one deity to another, hence the devotee must shift also or resume his normal personality. In either case the possession reflects an acute, situation specific sensitivity to highly arousing, sustaining, ceremonial cues. When they cease the possessed person loses his captive audience and supportive circumstances, and is left to his own devices. The deity usually leaves, but if related deities are coming he may remain in a semi-inappropriate state, which is tolerated if he behaves (Ravenscroft 1965: 173).

Gill and Brenman state that throughout hypnosis the subject maintains an appreciation of the total reality situation by means of a degree of normal ego functioning, including normal processes of perception, thought, motility, and unconscious defenses. The degree of change in reality orientation varies with the depth of hypnosis, the subject's personality, and other yet unknown factors. Some evidence of reality attunement is always present. If not, communication with the hypnotist would, of necessity, entirely disappear, which rarely even temporarily happens (1959: 101-102). Of course, in possession it is probably easier for this total lack of contact with reality to come about since there is no actual, unique external hypnotist with whom to maintain contact for direction and guidance. Part of the hypnotist function is provided by the different reality, the idea of the deity, furnished by the cultural patterns internalized by the possessed individuals. In most cases, however, the people who have become gods must remain constantly aware of reality because they must interact with each other as gods in what Louis Mars (1966: 22) refers to as an 'ethnodrama'.

The degree to which a subject does not follow the hypnotist's directives is a direct measure of his still-operating normal ego functioning, including defenses and reality adaptation (Gill and Brenman 1959: 35-36). Although a person under hypnosis actually does have a greater sense of personal responsibility and more capacity to make spontaneous efforts of will than is generally believed, his relative loss of such ego functions is a central aspect of the hypnotic state. The subject has thus both abdicated his sense of voluntary I-ness, and continued sporadic and fluctuating attempts to maintain himself as a separate person who can make independent efforts at will. Passive waiting for directions is perhaps the most singularly distinguishing characteristic of a hypnotic subject. Subjects told to do as they please usually wander aimlessly, say they do not want to do anything, and ask what they should do (Gill and Brenman 1959: 35-37, 41). The power of logical thinking can easily be lost during trance states, but can be maintained if required by the hypnotist (Bowers et al. 1961: 281). The reason for this is that the desire to abdicate total responsibility and voluntary effort is greater than the desire to control the situation oneself. In an emergency the hypnotized person could probably reassume responsibility as necessary, as can sometimes be done under the influence of alcohol or some drugs, when the desire to behave in a certain way is a very important determinant of behavior.

Gill and Brenman consider hypnosis to be an example of regression in the service of the ego, and I would extend this characterization to most forms of possession. Under certain conditions the ego regulates its own capacity to regress, relinquishing certain organizing functions of the ego, including the function of volition, in order to later gain improved control (1959: 159-160, 168). Regression in the service of the ego is (1959: 165):

1. more likely to occur as the ego grows more adaptive and less as the ego grows less so,
2. marked by a definite beginning and end,
3. reversible with a sudden and total reinstatement of the usual organization of the psyche,
4. terminable under emergency conditions by the subject unaided,
5. subject to occurrence only when the individual judges circumstances to be safe,
6. a state which is voluntarily sought by the subject and, in contrast to regression proper, active rather than passive.

All these factors also characterize traditionally regulated ceremonial possession.

The difference between regression proper and regression in the service of the ego is a matter of degree. In regression proper the over-all ego is changed, suffering a decrease in autonomy from both the id and the environment. In regression in the service of the ego a subsystem of the ego has been formed and it shows varying degrees of diminished autonomy from both id and environment. Certain phenomena characteristic of both processes are superficially similar, but vastly different in actual dynamics. For example, many phenomena in hypnosis look like id manifestations, e.g., the capacity to hallucinate, and access to repressed material, but they are very different from similar manifestations in cases of regression proper such as in schizophrenia. In regression in the service of the ego id-like phenomena are produced by a subsystem which hallucinates and recalls repressed material, rather than by the total ego system. Access to this repressed material is integrated with the subsystem, not with the overall ego system. This is evident in the fact that repressed material elucidated in hypnosis is not ordinarily accessible to the ego once the hypnotic state is terminated. In regression proper the id, ego, and superego are all altered, whereas in regression in the service of the ego only part of the ego is altered and it engages in altered interpersonal relations (Gill and Brenman 1959: 192-193, 196).

This explanation coincides well with Haitian folk theory. In possession the 'gros-bon-ange', the soul in charge of affect and cognition, is displaced by a Loa. The 'petit-bon-ange', or guardian angel, remains in its normal capacity. Thus there is a change in part of the possessed person's soul system, but although part of it relinquishes control of the individual, the other part remains vigilant. An analogous process takes place in dreaming. The 'gros-bon-ange' leaves the body, and its adventures constitute dreams. If anything happens to seriously disturb the 'petit-bon-ange', which always remains in contact with reality in both sleep and possession, the person will become seriously ill and will die if the situation is not corrected.

One of Gill and Brenman's central proposals is that in hypnosis a subsystem is established within the ego. It is a regressed system in the service of the over-all ego, and has control of some or all of the body's apparatuses. This subsystem alone is under the control of the hypnotist and by virtue of this control the hypnotist can direct and control the subject's apparatuses. The over-all ego also maintains a relationship with the hypnotist, a non-hypnotic, reality-oriented relationship. The ego relinquishes control of this subsystem to the hypnotist only temporarily and tentatively, and at any time can take it back. Such a capacity for adaptive regression in the service of the ego involving the temporary loss of autonomy of an ego subsystem ultimately increases the relative strength and well-being of the over-all ego (1959: 185, 191).

In the induction phase of hypnosis derivatives of the id appear, such as spontaneous outbursts of affect, accessibility to motility of previously repressed urges, the appearance of ideational representations of such urges in consciousness, evidence of archaic ego states in the alterations of body image and sensations, and depersonalization phenomena. This releasing of what appears to be previously repressed material indicates a weakening of the relative autonomy of the ego from the id, giving evidence that the synthetic functioning of the ego is being interfered with. The ego has asymmetrical relative autonomies since this domination by the id will give way to domination by the environment, as mainly created by and focused upon the hypnotist, in the fixed hypnotic state (Gill and Brenman 1959: 189-190).

The induction period represents the struggles of the ego to find a motivational pattern in conformity with its new reality. However, with experience in going into hypnosis, these induction phenomena disappear. The established state becomes automatized, that is, the previously ad hoc correspondence of motivational pattern and external pressure has become organized into an ego subsystem that can come into play on cue. The struggle to establish such a correspondence need not be repeated. The relative rapidity with which hypnosis can then be induced suggests that the elements which will become organized into the subsystem are available and ready to fall into place (Gill and Brenman 1959: 199-200).

It is the synthetic force of the ego which can build this new total unity including a regressed subsystem. Regression in the service of the ego is evidence of a strong rather than a weak ego since the ego has the capacity to regress in part while the depth and duration of this regression are controlled by the ego as a whole. The over-all ego must be sufficiently secure in its ultimate mastery to permit an apparent loss of control. Only a strong ego can allow the emergence of a good deal of repressed material, of which there is access to much more in hypnosis than in a normal state, while retaining sufficient energy to erect counter-cathexes against the upsurge of even more deeply repressed contents. This conclusion makes more understandable the fact of the higher incidence of hypnotizability in normal as opposed to neurotic subjects. The neurotic, with precarious defenses, can not spare any of the countercathectic energy holding down primitive instinctual impulses to use it to aid the over-all ego in building such a subsystem (Gill and Brenman 1959: 198, 215).

There are cases in which hypnosis is possible despite severe psychiatric illness. Perhaps these are instances in which the countercathexis against primitive instinctual drives is loosely held and easily yielded and the amount of countercathectic energy necessary to hold the over-all ego in abeyance is less. Hysterics are the easiest neurotics to hypnotize, probably because their particular ways of deploying countercathectic energy make energy shifts easier in them than in other neurotics (Gill and Brenman 1959: 217-218). Perhaps this latter fact in some measure accounts for the fact that in the past, and still to some extent, people who became possessed were usually described as hysterics. A greater part of this tendency is attributable to lack of knowledge about possession. Also it is quite feasible that there may be similarities in ego dynamics in hysteria and possession. The former would be dominated more by id pressure and the latter by environmental pressure, or by a culturally approved integration of both pressures. However, in possession situations in which cultural control is relaxed or nonexistent, id impulses come to the fore, making the two phenomena more similar. The findings of the Haitian psychiatrist, Emerson Douyon (1964), supply particularly good evidence of this trend for possession to be a manifestation of neurotic tendencies rather than culturally determined role playing, as cultural directives and controls break down.

It is my contention that in a culturally controlled situation with a coherent religious system to provide structure and content, possession by gods or spirits is a phenomenon of regression in the service of the ego. In less controlled situations the regression in the service of the ego approaches regression proper as id dominance takes precedence over environmental or cultural dominance.

According to Gill and Brenman's formulations, the most significant element in regression in the service of the ego, in terms of personality dynamics, is that a subsystem is temporarily set up in the ego to which the ego temporarily relinquishes control of the functioning of the organism (1959: 185). This ego subsystem is analogous to the personality of the deity in possession. The individual's executive faculties are temporarily placed in abeyance as the deity takes over such habitual functions. When the possession is ended the devotee is again himself with ordinarily no recollection of what has happened. It is suggested by some observers that after this probably very fulfilling experience the devotee is better adjusted to himself and to others.

The initial possession is wild and chaotic because the deity has not yet been tamed or socialized. The taming of the deity by means of a baptism, and an initiation process in which the devotee learns to serve him and fulfill his wants, is analogous to the working out, in hypnosis or regression in the service of the ego, of an established subsystem which corresponds to the new situational demands. As the early induction periods in hypnosis represent a disorganization of, and an ad hoc attempt to reorganize the functioning of the ego, the early violent induction phenomena in possession reflect the attempt to mutually adjust the god and his devotee to each other. Mischel says that the initial possession may be particularly erratic because two or more deities may be vying for the devotee's services. The priest must determine which deity should prevail (1957: 51). This vying represents the conflict between two possible subsystem configurations, both striving for expression. As the god is 'seated' or the subsystem established, a calmer and different personality ensues. As the frequently hypnotized person acquires a greater facility for going into hypnosis because his ego subsystem is readily available to be invoked, the experienced devotee becomes his god easily because the whole god personality is just waiting to be assumed on cue. The god personality has become shaped to fit the particular specifications of the personality of the devotee. In the atmosphere of the religious ceremony the suggestion becomes so strong that the deity becomes a real force which imposes itself upon the devotee.

The deity's personality is not unique to any one devotee because a number of people are possessed by the same god. The image of the god whose characteristics he will personify, the ego subsystem which will control his behavior, has come to the devotee for the most part from outside of himself. According to Maximilien, the devotee, from childhood, undergoes a discipline, accumulating day after day from his immediate environment a series of reactions and sensory-motor reflexes which give him a particular consciousness of his religion. He constructs within himself images of the deities which constitute a mystical thought system completely integrated into his personality. This thought system can be exteriorized with regularity under the proper circumstances. The manifestation is so precise that observers can identify the deity who has possessed the devotee. The devotee, rather than having defenses against such a reorganization of the ego, has instincts which create in him optimum conditions for receptivity to it. His religious beliefs give him a particular interest in attaining such a state (1945: 60, 62). If the individually personalized version of the god personality manifest by each devotee is seen as a compromise formation between the culturally determined expectations of how a particular deity is supposed to act, and behavioral proclivities the individual can not express under normal situations, it is evident that the devotee also has a strong psychological impetus to become possessed.

In regression proper the loss of ego autonomy is followed by dominance of either the id or the environment, whereas in regression in the service of the ego the loss of autonomy from both is a matter of degree. In possession, neither the id nor the environment can totally dominate. If the id were to do so the individual would not be acting out the personality of the god, but only his own libidinal impulses. This is evidently not the case in culturally controlled possession because observers are immediately aware of which god is present. If the environment were to dominate totally, all of the manifestations of a particular deity would be the same rather than distinct according to the personality characteristics of the particular devotee. This decreased autonomy characteristic of regression in the service of the ego is apparent in the increased freedom of expression of basic impulses plus increased susceptibility to suggestions from the environment. In this case the term environment must include the internalized image of the god personality as well as the actual external environment provided by the priest, other possessed participants, and spectators. As cultural control over possession lessens, the expression of basic impulses assumes a more dominant role, yet the regression may still be in the service of the ego, since some patterns, though perhaps very vague and general, still exist. The possession, though more idiosyncratic than culturally patterned in content, may still aid the devotee to maintain his psychological well-being because it provides him with a periodic release of pent-up tension and emotion.

The similarity of manifestation in regression proper and regression in the service of the ego, and the tending of each toward the other, can account for the relationship in folk theory between spirit possession and insanity. Most groups see these phenomena as related, but ultimately distinguishable. According to Gill and Brenman, what began as regression in the service of the ego may get out of hand and become regression proper (1959: 218). The initial symptoms of insanity and the call to serve the gods, particularly for one destined to be a priest, are often identical, and it is believed that a person who does not heed the call will go insane. Also, what begins as regression proper can perhaps be channeled and stabilized as the culturally constituted and valued god personality patterns give support to the weak or potentially weak ego.

The most important factor which distinguishes regression in the service of the ego from regression proper then seems to be the subsystem established in the former which takes over when the ego relinquishes control. In the societies under consideration, the religious system provides numerous ready-made subsystems which can be used as patterns for one's regression. Also, the gods provide objects of transference which allow this regression to occur in direct relationship to an authority figure, in this case really omnipotent because he is a god and not a man, hence giving the possessed person the security felt by a hypnotisand. He may feel exalted even more than secure because he is performing the supreme act in his religious belief system. He can also completely depend upon the community, hence his experience can not get out of hand and is useful for all. Knowledge that one is fulfilling such an important function vis-à-vis both the gods and the community probably gives one's ego added strength.

Until or unless a person's regressive symptoms are coordinated with one of these subsystems provided by his culture for the temporary restructuring of his ego, he has neither guidelines nor security in his regression, and it can get out of control. There seem to be two general reasons, psychological and socio-cultural, for not participating in this culturally patterned method of regression. The people who show the symptoms but never socialize them by responding to the gods are probably severely neurotic or psychotic, having such idiosyncratic understandings and attitudes that they can not adapt them to the culturally prescribed patterns. People who are socially and culturally distant from the milieu where possession behavior is the norm have no culturally approved method of regressing or of acting out their desires and fantasies, thus their gratification of such needs can only be done idiosyncratically.

According to Gill and Brenman, a person's hypnotizability is largely a constant matter. Variations in hypnotists, atmosphere, and even the use of drugs do not change the situation. The most suggestive data concerning differential hypnotizability comes from an analysis of the meaning of hypnosis to the subjects, but the authors have arrived at no conclusive results in this area. In some people hypnosis can be induced quickly and simply by an invitation to regress without any manipulation of their reality orientation. These are people in whom the ego subsystem must already exist and be ready to be triggered into action. A regressed interpersonal relationship with the hypnotist is the sine qua non. Once it is established, the regressed state is inevitable. Initial alterations in the subject's state of consciousness may, on the other hand, fail to develop into a full scale hypnotic state (1959: ix-xv, 196-197).

It has been pointed out in the previous chapter that in many cases mental concentration or strong suggestion can prevent the initial neurophysiological results of sonic driving from leading to possession or an altered state of consciousness, just as such factors can precipitate its advent. This process can be clearly observed in possession. People may be seen resisting the initial neuro-physiological impetus of possession by various means, and they may be successful. However, once the god comes into their heads they can no longer resist. In this context the god is the equivalent of both the invitation to regress and the figure accepting responsibility for the devotee. One must, of course, avoid reifying this god when comparing him to the hypnotist because the god is a cultural concept in combination with an aspect of the individual's personality, which is manifest under certain conditions. The god-as-hypnotist is thus an abstraction, an internalized cultural pattern, but one which is concretely real for the devotees, and which fulfills most of the functions of an actual hypnotist. The others are fulfilled by the priest and members of the community.

The good hypnotic subject is one who is most prone to give up his sense of freedom and will on both the ego and superego levels. He feels no embarrassment or guilt for anything he does because he has abdicated all responsibility for himself. It is easier to distinguish a poor subject than a good one according to shared personality traits. It is easier to distinguish those personality characteristics which seem to interfere with hypnosis than those which provide a favorable setting. Some factors which interfere with hypnotizability are general negativism, evasiveness, truculence, minimal capacity for emotional adaptiveness, and above all a striking effort to deny passive needs. People who are unable to engage in free and deep participation in human relationships are the poorest subjects. It is also difficult or impossible to hypnotize individuals characterized by marked obsessive or compulsive tendencies, an inclination to use projection as a major defense mechanism, overt aggressiveness or emotional unadaptability, or narcissism. These characteristics are infrequent in good subjects, who are more often characterized by strong repressive tendencies. They tend to reach out to the hypnotist for aid and comfort. Many also tend to exploit their feelings in a somewhat histrionic manner. The authors could not pin down positive indications of a high capacity for 'free participation' (1959: 43, 80-83).

It must be remembered that the subjects with whom Gill and Brenman had contact were members of American, or at least Western society, in which trance states are not generally valued. Some of the Haitian women studied by Douyon have many of the characteristics which Gill and Brenman say make bad hypnotic subjects, yet they are frequently possessed. They live in a milieu where possession is common, encouraged, and valued, and other personality characteristics they have apparently override those which would otherwise make them bad hypnotic subjects, if Gill and Brenman's classifications can be said to be universal, which is perhaps not the case. For example, most of the women studied by Douyon do not have satisfactory interpersonal relationships and are closer to the Loa for this very reason, believing that they can only depend upon the Loa. Because of their life situations they also tend to be quite negative, but possession is a very positive spot in their lives. Thus the cultural attitude of a society toward trance states would seem to be a more important determinant of hypnotizability than specific personal characteristics, as would the general types of personality configurations engendered by the child socialization process. Such factors would account for differences in hypnotizability between populations. Specific studies would then be necessary to determine if there are characteristics which universally make for a proclivity for such states, and if so, what they are and how they relate to specific cultural norms.

The good subject, again according to Gill and Brenman, has an intense unconscious need to be passively and aggressively demanding, but these needs are rarely expressed directly. They are usually defended against by denial and often by strong reaction formations. In hypnosis such individuals frequently revert nostalgically to a phase of life in which passive-receptive mastery was the major means of coping with the outside world, when their security was achieved by participation in a greater unit, the all-powerful parent (1959: 83-84). Such characteristics are common to both the Balinese and the Haitian peasants, as will be seen in the chapter on socialization. In possession the subject can both participate in the omnipotent god image and achieve passive and aggressive mastery over the whole community of spectators. He is totally dependent upon them but they must accede to his every wish because he is now a god.

It is not enough to say that a good hypnotic subject is one with intense regressive longings because many people with these longings have defense mechanisms which in strength or quality prevent such regression from coming about. In a good subject the pull toward regression is offset in a fluid way by a complex of defense operations poised in a delicate balance, which is such that a hypnotist's intervention can tip it. Susceptibility to hypnosis seems then to be essentially the outcome of a particular kind of drive-defense-adaptation balance. This resulting balance may be the same even where the content and relative strength of these three variables is different (Gill and Brenman 1959: 84, 137). Therefore, it is to be expected that people susceptible to hypnosis, and possession, will have very different characters, their significant common trait being a particular type of balance in their personality dynamics.

Occasionally a good hypnotic subject will show all signs of going into hypnosis before the hypnotist has tried to bring about changes in the subject's bodily awareness. Such a person's usually unconscious wish to go into hypnosis is so overwhelming that the process of loosening his reality moorings is unnecessary. Such instances of spontaneous hypnosis can take place at the time of the hypnotic session or outside of it. In the former case the patient suddenly gives every appearance of being under hypnosis and/or reports all of the subjective sensations usually accompanying his own characteristic hypnotic state, in the absence of any direct suggestion from the hypnotist or even in direct opposition to his stated wish. Such spontaneous states come upon the good subject when his attempts at active mastery are failing. Such failure usually arises in situations of extreme stress or anxiety and may be sufficient to invoke the image of the hypnotist and all of the subjective sensations of the usual hypnotic state. This spontaneous hypnosis is similar in motivation to the change in depth of hypnosis previously mentioned. This regressive state is not simply less adaptive. It may be seen as an attempt to increase adaptation when the organism meets environmental stress with which it can not cope or to which it can not adapt. It regresses to a level of more primitive adaptive organization as though in the hope of magically reinstating an earlier form of organism-environment relationship. Such regression is frequently maladaptive since the environment is likely to resist such efforts at magical manipulation (Gill and Brenman 1959: 29, 66-67, 84, 101, 208-209).

In some of the areas under consideration, most notably Haiti, we find possession outside of the normal ceremonial occasions and without any ceremonial atmosphere. Such non-ceremonial possession occurs in specific kinds of social and psychological circumstances usually involving extreme personal stress, fear, pain, or fatigue, or when the honor, interest, or life of the subject is threatened. These situations are usually such that they require independence, assertiveness, dominance, or responsibility beyond the capacity of most Haitian peasants. When the peasant finds himself in a social or private situation which demands mastery beyond his normal resources, or which threatens his personal adequacy, he may become possessed by a Loa. It is usually his principal Loa, or 'maît' tête' (master of the head) who comes to help. Spontaneous possessions may occur when arguments become too heated, rural busses crash, a wife is beaten by her husband, a parent dies leaving his son to take over the family, a peasant must take a long and arduous journey, and similar trying circumstances. People may also become possessed when exceptional physical effort, endurance, or cunning is required. In the possessed state the individual has an incredible range of physical capacity and endurance relative to his unpossessed performance. Louis Mars observed an operation in a Port-au-Prince hospital during which the patient suffered horribly because of insufficient anaesthesia. The patient began singing a Vodun song and as the pain increased his formerly grimacing face became serene as he was possessed by his 'maît' tête'. The operation ended in complete calm (1948: 1077).

Such situations are a challenge to the Haitian peasant's evaluation of his own adequacy and put a strain on his psychic economy. The culturally dictated response is to rely on the gods in such times of stress. The socialization process engenders dependence on these powers stronger than man to do something or to possess the devotee so that he may, in the guise of the god, cope with the situation. The peasant, as a part of his traditional heritage, expects such direct intervention by his principal deity in severe crisis or conflict situations (Ravenscroft 1965: 179).

The individual who is possessed in a stress situation feels no fear, and his assumption of the personality of the god immediately elevates him to a position superior to that of anyone with whom he is forced to interact. He is no longer even himself, but is the god. This is true provided, of course, that the others present subscribe to the same traditions and values. As a god he is granted social license, and his position relative to everyone else, plus his increased ability, allow him to master the situation or leave it without losing face. Whatever he does will be attributed to the god, not to himself (Ravenscroft 1965: 179).

Such non-ceremonial possession usually comes very discretely, without the usual convulsive induction period (Price-Mars 1928: 130). This is probably in part so, as is probably also the case in spontaneous hypnosis, because of the absence of sensory deprivation or bombardment and its neurophysiological responses. Such non-ceremonial possession is less frequent than ceremonial possession and it is rare that any other than one's principal deity will come. According to Ravenscroft, this fact indicates the importance of the altered consciousness of reality in producing possession (1965: 179-180). The ceremonial atmosphere is apparently quite important in causing the advent of possession. A person expects help from his principal deity and in such spontaneous situations there is not a high enough level of arousal, as would exist in a ceremony, to bring on the gods who come with less ease than the principal deity. In other words, the individual may have a number of ego subsystems or god personalities corresponding to different needs, which may be manifest at different times; but one, his principal deity, is dominant and is manifest most easily. It is also likely that the principal deity is the one most intimately concerned with the life of the devotee, and for that reason he would be the deity most apt to respond in times of stress. The information on the Zar cult in Ethiopia, on the contrary, suggests that one may be possessed by a different Zar according to the demands of the situation. There is also, however, more tendency to fake possession, or to accuse others of doing so in the Zar cult than in Haiti or the other areas. Thus one may merely pretend to become the Zar most convenient for the circumstances of the moment.

The absence of such spontaneous possession in Bahia is perhaps related to the fact that the religion is more tightly structured than in Haiti with a more coherent mythology, and individuals mold themselves more to the personalities of the deities rather than interpreting the latter to fit their own tendencies, although they do inject elements of their own personalities. Also, since Bahia is a culturally mixed, urban area, rather than a homogeneous rural area, where everyone is not involved in the same belief system, such behavior would be socially dysfunctional. The socialization process undoubtedly develops personalities which are less dependent and more able to deal with stressful situations than in Haiti — people who can summon up their own energy, rather than to rely on possession by their deity, to cope with their problems. Essentially this means that they can consciously face trouble and accept the responsibility for dealing with it with the best resources they have at their disposal, rather than to attribute any response they make to some supernatural, but actually unconscious, source. Also the Loa seem to be a much more intimate part of the everyday life of the average Haitian peasant than are the Orisha in Bahia, since Haitians can even marry Loa and make business deals with them.

In corresponding situations of great stress in Bali people try to escape physically, but if this is impossible they withdraw by going into a deep sleep. If either alternative is impossible they behave in a completely irrational manner (Belo 1960). Their mechanism for dealing with stress does not allow them to cope with it, but rather to avoid coping with it. In Haiti, however, by becoming possessed one can actually deal effectively with such a situation. The socialization process does not condition the Haitian peasant to deal with these eventualities in his normal state, but provides cultural mechanisms by which he can mobilize his unconscious potentialities and make them work for him.

An important factor in hypnosis is the subject's motivation. Van der Walde considers hypnosis to be a goal-oriented phenomenon in which the subject hopes to achieve some desired end. This motivation is highly individual, dependent upon a variety of needs and desires. Most often it is a question of gratifying unacceptable wishes without superego or social censure. Gratification may be derived from one's own hypnotic behavior or from the dependent hypnotic relationship, or both. It is actually the subject, not the hypnotist, who prescribes the extent and expression of the wishes gratified in hypnosis. In order for a hypnotic suggestion to have sufficient motive power to bring results it must correspond to an intense, usually unconscious, wish on the part of the subject (van der Walde 1968: 61).

Belo notes that people classified as trancers sometimes demonstrate an ability to stay out of the trance state at will in the presence of all the stimuli which usually call it forth, giving evidence that the trance is something to which the subject must give himself up. The stimuli bringing about the trance are not so much stimuli to be followed by mechanical responses as factors in a setting favorable to inducing a trance state in those who are willing to assume it. For example, in Bali, men who are usually kris dancers act as assistants and help the entranced on days when they are not called to dance (1960: 150). In the other areas also it is apparent that people make deliberate acts of will to bring on their possessions or to resist their advent.

Increased motivation and role-playing in line with the subject's understanding of the demand characteristics of the situation are major determinants of the content of hypnotic behavior (Orne 1959; Sarbin 1950; White 1941). White states that hypnotic behavior can only be adequately described and understood if seen as meaningful, goal-directed striving. He considers the most general goal to be that of behaving like a hypnotized person as this is defined by the operator and understood by the subject (1941: 483-484).

The subject usually knows, or thinks he knows, the demand characteristics of the hypnotic state, and they, rather than any other variables, more reasonably account for the actual content of his behavior than the effects of his altered state of consciousness (Orne 1959: 277, 284). Experiments have shown that a subject who believes, or is told, that people under hypnosis behave in certain ways or experience certain feelings or sensations, will tend to behave in these ways or experience these sensations although this is not really typical hypnotic behavior and has no basis in the trance phenomenon per se (Orne 1959). Non-ceremonial possession in Haiti and spontaneous hypnotic states are instances in which the hypnotic or possession state is mainly a very highly motivated response to a set of well-known demand characteristics, with this element most likely overriding the influence of an altered state of consciousness. Also, sometimes there are people in ceremonies who seem not to be actually possessed although they are going through the motions. Such behavior is frequently less a case of deliberate faking than a highly

motivated attempt to respond to the known characteristics of the state
by people who, for some reason, are not in an actual trance.

The subject is so motivated to conform to the demand
characteristics of the situation, as he understands them or as the
hypnotist suggests, because of his special relationship with the
hypnotist. His characteristic increased suggestibility is a result of his
great motivation to conform to the wishes of the hypnotist. The
subject's apparent increase in physical strength and endurance, as
well as local anaesthesia,[1] are a result of great motivation and can
actually be produced in a normal state if the motivational level can be
raised sufficiently.

White indicates that hypnotic subjects make substantial additions
to what is stated in the hypnotist's suggestions. He considers this an
element differentiating automatic, purely responsive behavior from
goal-directed striving to behave like a person under hypnosis. Also,
the post-hypnotic suggestions to which they respond may be vague,
leaving the subjects to fill in the details of execution. The subjects
thus play an active, discriminating role. They are not automatons
(1941: 484-485).

In possession, the god personality assumed corresponds to some
aspect of the possessed person's personality, which is probably not
expressed in his normal everyday behavior. The possessed person can
gratify the need to express these unexpressed facets of himself while
at the same time playing a role of great importance to the
community. Everyone is familiar with the demand characteristics of
the personality of each god, but many gods have several different
facets corresponding to what sometimes amount to almost
diametrically opposed character types. Also it is recognized that each
person has his own style of becoming his god so that one god may be
manifest in a variety of ways. The general outline is provided by
tradition but each individual inserts his own personality to provide
substance. The possessed person does behave according to what he
believes are the demand characteristics of his new role, but they
merely give him a skeleton which he must clothe.

Besides fulfilling unconscious needs and exhibiting hidden aspects
of his personality, the devotee consciously desires to become a god to

---

[1] This does not contradict what was said in the previous chapter about the
anaesthetic effects of rhythmic stimulation. The two elements are more likely to be
mutually reinforcing.

escape his regular earthly lot for a while and to participate in a more meaningful, more pleasant level of reality. He is the center of attention and gains great prestige. He is performing a culturally valued service by pleasing one of the gods who regulates the life of the community. With such great motivation people dance for long hours on end without tiring, and perform feats which their physical capabilities would never permit under normal circumstances.

Hypermnesia [abnormally complete memory or recall] is a classic phenomenon of hypnosis, resulting in part from the relaxation of defenses, particularly repression (Gill and Brenman 1959: 49). Heightened recall is also the result of a highly motivated response to suggestion (White 1941: 480). Possession may also be characterized by hypermnesia, which is seen as evidence of the deity's omniscience. Ravenscroft notes that the possessing deity remembers his own activities during previous possessions as well as the devotee's daily unpossessed behavior. When a deity is possessing a person he is also familiar with the past behavior of any other gods who may have possessed this person. Thus the deities have access to the recall of all the devotee's behavior in any state of consciousness. The deity may behave in a manner alien and threatening to the devotee personally and socially and not at all in tune with the person's previous behavior in a normal state or when possessed by another deity (1965: 160-161).

In his normal state the devotee is not supposed to remember anything at all from his possessed state. From most reports it is apparently true that in general people do not remember. In some places they are not to be told about their behavior, and in others they are told and may be shocked and sometimes chagrined at these revelations. Orne says that the post-hypnotic amnesia which appears superficially to be a complete wiping out of the memory for the hypnotized period is by no means complete. This is evidenced in post-hypnotic suggestion. The subject denies any recall yet persists in the suggested behavior (1959: 283).

White says that it is not that the subject can not remember, but that he can not make the effort of sustaining the activity of remembering. The striving to remember is inhibited by antagonistic striving to act as if the trance is forgotten, which is perceived as the correct behavior for a hypnotic subject (1941: 491). It seems also that forgetting all that went on in the hypnotic period is probably one of the conditions for successful hypnosis, because the only way to completely deny any responsibility for what went on is not to remember. Not remembering afterward is probably as important as not being responsible during hypnosis in allowing the subject to let down his defenses and be truly free in his self-expression. The same holds true in possession.

It is within the logic of the system that the devotee not remember what happened during the possessed state since he was no longer himself but had become a deity who was responsible for everything done. The devotee can not remember because he was not there. The Orisha, Vodun, Loa, Zar, or Holey was in his body controlling his behavior and the soul which usually performed this duty was absent. To remember what was done in possession would be for the devotee to admit to himself and others that he was not really possessed. His identity and personality were not really replaced by the deity's. The ritual would thus have no meaning if people thought that the mythical beings whose manifestations constitute its purpose and who are the substance of the community's belief system were not really present (Leiris 1958: 86-87). To remember one's behavior would be tantamount to saying, given the content of the belief system, that the deities did not really have the power to possess their devotees, thus the gestures of the devotees would be mere drama rather than religious ritual.

The degree of actual forgetfulness varies from society to society. In all of them the devotees are not supposed to remember according to cultural dicatates, and therefore most probably do not because they believe they can not. Of course if this dichotomy between the individual and his deity were as sharp as it is said to be there would be no need for a devotee to be shocked and chagrined as some are. In Haiti, according to most accounts, the devotee apparently has no memory or responsibility at all and his possession is spoken of as if totally unrelated to him, in contrast with Bahia where people are often surprised and upset at their possessed behavior. Devotees of the Zar cult sometimes, contrary to the stated ideal, do seem to remember their possessed behavior as evidenced in their subsequent actions (Leiris 1958: 77). Of course such action may be unconsciously motivated as in post-hypnotic suggestion, rather than conscious remembering of the possessed state, and this must exist for all of the societies, but it is defined differently among the Zar devotees. Zar devotees can also, as previously mentioned, describe how they felt when possessed, and do speak of their possessed behavior in the first person. They thus may be blamed for what was done by the Zar, since the Zar and his devotee are not considered as distinct as in the other societies.

There is thus a very important difference between the Zar cult and the other groups in respect to their actual, as opposed to idealized, attitudes toward what really happens in possession and what the relationship between a devotee and his deity really is. In the Zar cult, as opposed to the others, the Zar does not enter the person's body because it is so strong that it would kill him. It just rests on his shoulders like a body carried on a person's back. Therefore the soul is not fully expelled, as is the Haitian 'gros-bon-ange', but the Zar joins it in the body and subjugates it (Leiris and de Heusch — discussion in de Heusch 1965: 165-166). Hence there is an implicit understanding that it is not a mythical being who is acting, but a human being in a state very different from the normal but not really as distinct as the change in name and supposed change of status would seem to indicate. Thus the theoretical doctrine says that the Zar personality is substituted for the devotee's, but in actuality this substitution is not seen as complete. The verbs used for the Zar's takeover are most frequently 'seize', 'capture', 'appropriate', and similar ideas (Leiris 1958: 78).

This difference in native formulation of the actual process of possession accounts for why the Zar devotees can better remember their possessions and are more responsible for their behavior. It also accounts for why there is more faking and accusation of faking in the Zar cult than in the other groups, as well as why faking is less reprehensible. Leiris says that since there are so many accusations of faking among devotees who are hardly skeptics, they must have personal experience of their own faking or of that by others which did not fool them. Such evidence of faking does not seem to disturb the basic belief in the authenticity of possession. Although there may be points of contestation, the whole ensemble is never questioned (1958: 90-91).

It would seem that if the devotees do experience true possession at times, they would have no reason to question the total ensemble because of occasional faking in themselves and others. Their experience of the real thing is proof that it exists. The only reason for questioning the entire ensemble would be if all possessions were merely theatrical, which is obviously not the case since there is a definite distinction between the real and the fake.

The difference in relationship between the devotee and his Zar also in part accounts for the greater degree of faking and its lack of reprehensibility. Faking is a matter of degree of relative control between the individual's personality and the Zar, since they cohabit the individual's body. The presence and influence of the devotee's own personality does not mean that the Zar is not there, as it would in the other groups, but merely that it is not in full control. Since the relationship between the devotee and his Zar is more intimate and informal than between men and their deities in the other groups, perhaps the individual is less aware than he would be in the others of whether he is sincere or faking.

A very important factor to consider, which may explain this difference in tone of the devotee-deity relationship, is that the Zar are not the omnipotent gods of the community who control the workings of the universe. They seem to be more like spirits with human personalities and competences related to the workings of everyday human life. This contrasts with the Orisha, the Vodun, the original Haitian Loa, and the Holey, who are deities concerned with the forces of nature more than with everyday human concerns. This difference in the character of the deities is probably extremely important in defining the relationship between them and their devotees, and in accounting for the relative seriousness of faking their presence. A devotee who fakes the presence of one of these powerful nature deities is pretending to propitiate him in dancing for and sacrificing to him, but is not actually doing so since the god is not really present. This would seem to incur the god's wrath and bring about severe misfortune, perhaps for the individual's family and community in addition to himself.

The Zar are not as powerful as these great nature gods, nor are they concerned with anything really ultimate, since they are not the deities of the whole community, as will be touched upon later. Their manifestations seem to be occasions for them to enjoy themselves in a very human way, rather than occasions when men can re-enact the mythico-historical past of their community and communicate intimately with the deities who control both their personal lives and the well-being of the community as a whole. The nature of the deities is thus very important in determining what the mechanism of possession in a specific society will be like.

CHAPTER THREE

INITIATION

The West African religions involving possession and the traditional Afro-American religions have as an important characteristic the institution of initiation. It is during the initiation period, the duration of which varies with social conditions, that one acquires one's possessing deity and learns how to serve him. It is also during this period that the personality of the god is established as an ego subsystem of the devotee's, and the signals which trigger the manifestation of this subsystem are inculcated. It is true that at present initiation is becoming increasingly brief and less rigorous, and in some places no longer exists at all. In such situations people still know how to behave when becoming their gods because they have observed possession all of their lives. However, the possession phenomena are becoming less organized and individual idiosyncrasies are being allowed to replace cultural control.

The phenomenon that takes place in possession is the manifestation of a secondary personality in the possessed person. This personality, a product of the interaction of cultural patterns and individual personalities, is inculcated as a kind of conditioned reflex. Herskovits speaks of such a reflex as a psychological process developed in the terms of the norms of the culture, which is so internalized that it rarely becomes conscious. When the stimulus is given the response is automatic because the individual has become habituated to a pattern in which he sees nothing abnormal. In a cultural milieu in which people believe in numerous anthropomorphic deities and where from childhood a person is taught that he will be able to receive a god at the call of the drums, it is probable that as a result of these factors, in the proper situation, the response will come. He will be possessed (Verger 1954: 327).

Verger probes into the process by which a person who will be possessed acquires the reflexes and stimuli which condition this tendency. He rejects the idea that the people involved may be neurotic, suggesting rather that the effect must be similar to hypnotic somnambulism with a doubling of the personality. Auto-suggestion replaces suggestion from an outside source and such manifestations correspond to real individual behavioral tendencies revived from the depths of the unconscious during initiation (1954: 336-337).

Initiation in such religions does not consist, contrary to general belief, of primarily a solemn revelation of esoteric knowledge. It is rather the creation in the initiate of a second, and secondary personality and the inculcation of behavior conforming to certain traditional models. The initiate must acquire a totally new set of conditioned reflexes much at variance with his old ones. Since reflexes are not in the domain of reason they can best be acquired, in connection with appropriate stimuli, in a state in which consciousness is necessarily absent (Verger 1954: 337).

The initiation always begins with symbolic death, marking complete rupture with one's past life and personality, and ends with rebirth into a new life as a new person. During this period of seclusion from the everyday world, the novice is plunged into a state of lethargy, apparently becoming mentally debilitated and unable to reason as a result of the techniques used by the initiators. He is supposed to have forgotten everything. He does not know how to talk and can only express himself in inarticulate syllables. The restrictions imposed upon him for long periods of time cause such a state to actually come about. He is usually kept physically immobile, lying on a mat for days. Forbidden to talk to anyone he must signal his wants to an attendant by ringing a bell (Verger 1954: 337). Among the Songhay, when the initiate is taken out of the sanctuary to learn a dance step or something, he is totally covered. He is not considered to be there, his old self having died. Since the god has not yet come into him he is considered an 'empty horse' (Rouch 1960: 251). The novice, a vigorous young person, must be thus totally passive in the hands of experienced priests and devotees adept at psychological conditioning, who exert their wills and energy to remodel the novice's personality in the image of the deity the novice is to serve, and whom he should continually have in mind (de Heusch 1965: 154-155).

In such a state the initiate's mind is cleared of all previous memories, and the particular rhythms, songs, dances, colors, and all the behavior of the god are inculcated into the future devotee. A close association is established between stimuli and responses (Verger 1954: 337). An initial sacred bath in herbs which render one lethargic is very important in bringing on a tabula rasa state in the novice's mind. The herbs are supposed to make the person's body more easily permeable to his deity, and in Brazil possession usually comes on as a result of the herbal bath (Bastide 1953: 34). Leaves and herbs as used in baths are of extreme importance, their names and uses constituting the most secret part of the ritual. The vital force of the Orisha resides in them so no ceremony can take place without the use of them to render the initiate susceptible to possession. Devotees must have periodic herbal baths to maintain their links with the vital force of their Orisha (Verger 1954: 337-338).

Since this herbal bath renders one lethargic and is used before all ceremonies to make the gods come more easily, especially in Bahia, it seems quite likely that the people who are to be possessed may be experiencing the medicinal effects of the herbs when they arrive at the ceremony. Also it seems that in these periodic states of lethargy the individual would particularly concentrate on the image and the behavior of the god as impressed upon him in the lethargic state of the initiation period.

The method of inculcating the conditioned reflex of assuming the personality of a god under the proper circumstances is similar in a sense to the process of brainwashing. It would seem that the prolonged sensory deprivation and ideational limitation and concentration (the novice is supposed to focus totally on the idea of his god), plus the medicinal effect of the herbs, must be sufficient to create a condition of transmarginal inhibition in which the individual's cerebral slate is temporarily wiped clean. Also, since the initiate sincerely believes this to be the case, and is trying to behave as an initiate should, it probably is functionally true. In such a state the novice is very susceptible to suggestion, the perfect situation for him to learn a totally new, and highly desirable, behavior pattern. According to Sargant, once this pattern is learned, a slight stimulation reminiscent of the situation in which it was acquired can automatically set if off again, although at other times the person performs normally (1957: 15-16). This is precisely the phenomenon which occurs in ceremonial possession. When the initiate is reborn to a normal state he must relearn all of the everyday things he previously knew, such as walking, talking, eating, etc., since he is now a new person, often with a new name. Once he resumes his normal state, an herbal bath combined with the proper drum rhythm, atmosphere, and execution of the proper dance steps are sufficient to bring on the behavior of the god in him.

Verger compares the initiate to a photographic plate. He carries

within him the latent image of his god, impressed during initiation
on a mind freed of all impressions. This image is revealed and
manifest when all the favorable conditions are united. Each person
has several contradictory tendencies and faculties within his total
being, but for many reasons only some develop and form his
conscious personality. The initiation period makes another of these
personalities come to the fore. Thus, for a time, the devotee's
behavior is made to conform to that of one of the traditional deities
(Verger 1954: 338).

   Verger asserts that the initiate, upon coming out of the state of
lethargy of the initiation period, is almost never conscious of his
initiation. He has no memory of what has happened, but seemingly
is on the other side of an airtight partition separating two different
manifestations of his self (1954: 339). Similarly, as has been
mentioned, in some of the societies in question everyone is forbidden
to speak to a devotee of his possession, although in others this is
evidently not true since some people know what they have done and
are often embarrassed by their conduct. Verger found that in
traditional Candomblés in Bahia he had difficulty obtaining
permission to take photographs because the leaders were repulsed by
the idea that the devotee should see the image of 'the other'—his
personality as the god.[1]

   It is customary in Haiti not to discuss a person's possession with
him, in keeping with the clear distinction between a person's
conscious self and his Loa. A group of adepts may discuss the actions
of a Loa in great detail without thinking to make a single reference to
the person whose head the Loa entered. Deren specifically noted this
feature because people discussed her possession by Erzulie in her
presence, but only in terms of the authenticity of Erzulie's
manifestation. They did not refer to Maya Deren herself. It was from
such conversations that she gathered that her possession was
considered authentic and conformed to the pattern of activity that
would be expected of Erzulie (1953: 320).

   The initiation period may actually be seen as a kind of profound
hypnotic state in which a new set of stimuli and responses are
suggested by the religious officials in charge. These new responses

---

[1] Verger did take some pictures which are quite impressive. See: Verger,
Pierre—Mémoires d'IFAN # 51, 1957 or Verger—*Dieux d'Afrique*. The latter is the
same set of photos as the former without the text.

can be provoked in the future by the appropriate stimuli through the mechanism of post-hypnotic suggestion.

In Haiti there is often no initiation period, yet fidelity to tradition seems to be quite strong in the rural areas. In Bahia the cults with shorter or no initiation periods are not traditional and seem to be prey to fraud and general dissolution. This situation is most likely a result of the different social conditions. The main reason for eliminating or shortening initiation periods is usually economic. In rural Haiti the peasants live in close everyday relations with their gods. Some people actually have wedding services and are married to various Loa. It is also possible to make deals with the Loa assuring success in one's undertakings. The spontaneous possessions exhibit the proximity of the Loa, many of whom are thought to reside in local bodies of water. Children see not only the ceremonial possessions but also non-ceremonial possessions as people are pursuing their daily activities. Hence the relationship with the gods is extremely close and everyone is probably clearly aware of the specific behavior of each god and of all of the factors which bring him to the community in the body of a devotee.

In Bahia, however, the situation is more formal. First, the mythology of the traditional Candomblé is more complete, coherent, and complex than in Haiti, where the mythology has apparently become detached from its traditional African basis. This is partially due to the geographic dispersion of the Haitians in small, rural villages, whereas Salvador, Bahia is an urban center where traditional Candomblés have been concentrated because Africans were allowed to congregate more or less freely there. The official policies in Haiti and Brazil toward African religion and gatherings were diametrically opposed, although the reasoning behind both was the same. In Haiti the slaves were not allowed to congregate because the French feared they would rebel, which was, of course, true. Also an attempt was made to root out their religion because the whites were afraid of it.

In Brazil, however, the slaves were allowed to keep their religion and were specifically encouraged to congregate because it was felt that by gathering together frequently they would maintain an awareness of their traditional differences and not develop a common cause because of their present shared state. Also, contact between Brazil and Africa continued to a later date. Some black people went back to Africa, especially Nigeria, to be educated and initiated into the traditional religion, then returned to Brazil as priests with authentic knowledge. Hence Brazilian theology and mythology has remained more intact and complex.

In Haiti the mythology and theology have undergone changes commensurate with the changing social conditions. For example, new, purely Haitian deities corresponding to elements of Haitian life have been added to the Vodun pantheon, and traditional deities have changed their personalities. Also, ritual is much more important than mythology, and there is therefore less esoteric knowledge to be taught in initiation. In Brazil people are familiar with the Candomblé from frequent association and observation of ceremonies, but they need the initiation period to acquire an organized knowledge of the religion. They must learn the Yoruba terms and their meanings, understand the explanatory myths, and become familiar with their own privileges and obligations.

Bahia, as an urban area in contrast to the rural setting of Haitian Vodun, has more of a cultural mixture. The people involved in the Candomblé do not spend all of their time with other members and hence are less totally saturated with the singular kinds of beliefs held by the Haitian peasants. The Bahians seem to have a less intimate relationship with the Orisha, who must come from the mythical Guinea (Africa). They do not come for spontaneous possessions in moments of great stress as in Haiti, which is probably preferable in this culturally heterogeneous urban center, but do come to give warnings or advice. In the latter case it is not clear from the literature whether the devotee assumes the personality of the god or merely receives a message, although the latter possibility seems most reasonable. It does happen that people may get possessed on their way to a ceremony upon hearing the sound of their own drum rhythm, but they are specifically prepared to do so. This is analogous to ceremonial possession, although a bit premature, rather than to non-ceremonial possession in response to stress.

Because the Bahians do not live in as close everyday interaction with their deities as the Haitians, they probably have more need than the Haitians for such initiation periods in order to have the god personalities inculcated into them. It also seems, probably for the same reasons, that the Bahians need more concurrent elements to stimulate such possession than do the Haitians. The Haitians, for example, do not seem to attribute so much importance to the lethargy-inducing herbal baths. This difference in social milieu and consequent intimacy of relationship with the gods would seem to account, at least in part, for the fact that the lack of initiation has not led to the degeneration of rural Haitian religion as it has in Brazil.

In traditional Dahomey, where possession was much more a social than an individual phenomenon, in that an individual's Vodun was determined by his family background rather than by any personal characteristics, initiation lasted as long as seven years for some deities. Each pantheon had its own specifications. It is reasonable to assume that initiation must be more rigorous when the new personality is a purely social imposition rather than a complement to the devotee's own personality because in the latter case the individual is, to large extent, merely being himself.

CHAPTER FOUR

POSSESSION AND THE SOCIALIZATION PROCESS

In Bali, trance is a cultural form accessible to most people, but occurring in different proportions in different villages. In some villages everyone can be possessed at one time or another, even the smallest children. Belo reports an incident in which children as young as three years old were possessed in imitation of their elders. In the other cultures in question children are not possessed, as far as has been noted, although childhood dreams and incidents may indicate who their possessing deities will be.

Gill and Brenman (1959: 295) assume, along with Bateson and Mead (1942), that everyone in Bali has the capacity to go into a trance in response to specific social situations. P. M. Van Wulfften Palthe of the Psychiatric Service in Java states that only individuals who are highly emotional and have a somewhat infantile psychic structure can attain the state of reduced consciousness necessary for such a state (Belo 1960: 6). However, the prevalence of trance states and their importance in the culture seem to indicate that the conditions of personality development favor a personality structure quite susceptible to hypnotoform phenomena. A study of this personality structure would probably illuminate some of the features which give one a proclivity for altered states of consciousness, as well as the function trance phenomena can play in the successful adaptation of the personality. The Balinese socio-cultural system apparently fosters a personality structure containing certain habits and tendencies which cause a propensity for trance states. However, one can not assume that in any society of similar structure and with similar personality development, such trances will necessarily play an important and approved role in the society without empirical proof. Nor can one assume that different socialization processes will not lead to trance phenomena, as will be indicated by the comparison between Bali and Haiti. A number of cultural and personality factors must co-exist in a society where trance manifestations constitute an organized societal technique.

Gill and Brenman make three propositions concerning the Balinese trance (1959: 318):

1. The trance in Bali is a variety of hypnosis.

2. Balinese susceptibility is an integral aspect of the kind of personality and body image fostered by Balinese culture.

3. This kind of personality and body image in Bali present, in exaggerated form, the kind of personality structure and body image changes characteristic of hypnotizable people in Western society.

A comparative description of some of the major themes in Haitian and Balinese child-rearing practices should illustrate the manner in which some personality traits conducive to trance behavior are inculcated. However, the trance phenomena in Haiti and Bali are quite different, and correlations can be seen between some of the elements of child socialization and these differences. Brief illustrations from the Zar cult and the Songhay tribe suggest that there are indeed cross-cultural similarities in the personality structure and body image of persons susceptible to possession or hypnosis. A variety of physiological, psychological, and socio-cultural factors combine to produce a propensity for such states. Knowledge of these factors is very incomplete, so with no pretense of being exhaustive I shall illustrate briefly some of these factors as related to child socialization.

Bateson and Mead put great emphasis on the character of the mother-child relationship in Bali. The mother apparently stimulates the child greatly, then suddenly rejects it, eventually causing it to become unresponsive. This unresponsiveness engendered by child-rearing practices results in a character structure in which strong affective display occurs only under very special circumstances such as funerals, drama, and trances (1942). Ceremonial trances, particularly in the Witch and Dragon plays, give the entranced people, which number may eventually include the entire audience, an opportunity to rush madly about and express strong emotions which can not be expressed in everyday social interaction.

The unresponsive withdrawal of the Balinese is related to another characteristic — a widespread tendency to abstracted states or dissociation in the course of daily living. A mother and child will assume such abstracted states after active play, as will an artist after finishing his work. In crowds many faces can be seen which appear similarly unresponsive to the immediate environment (Bateson and Mead 1942). Gill and Brenman regard these states as abortive forms of trance, and their universal presence among the Balinese is important evidence for the authors' inference that almost all Balinese have the capacity to go into a trance. Another related characteristic which the authors see as supportive evidence is the manner in which the Balinese withdraw in deep but normal sleep as a defense against anxiety (1959: 29, 97).

There are thus two major forms of altered states of consciousness common in Balinese society — sleep as a withdrawal from anxiety-producing situations, and frequently hyperactive trances in which people release pent-up affect. These two types, which may be likened to stuporous and alert hypnotic states, have behavioral parallels in Balinese children who do not learn to be unresponsive soon enough in life. Girls have a series of violent temper tantrums. Boys have almost trance-like sulks and attacks of deep physical dependency in which they lie back against people or inanimate objects (Gill and Brenman 1959: 300-301).

The Balinese character is strikingly shot through with ceremony, ritual, and pageantry, which may be compared to the histrionic element in hypnosis. There would seem to be a close relationship between the outbursts of usually checked affect, which individuals often express in hypnosis, and the culturally prescribed expression of strong affect on ceremonial occasions. This would be particularly true in a society in which great affect is built up and then systematically denied expression (Gill and Brenman 1959: 300).

The teaching process in Bali puts much emphasis on the child's passivity and flexibility. As a baby he is not allowed to crawl, but is carried, often by a young child. As this child nurse frequently plays boisterously while carrying him, the baby must be flexible and relaxed, and adapt to the movements of his nurse's body in order to avoid unpleasant jolts. He even manages to sleep in a sling on the nurse's hip while she is having a temper tantrum (Bateson and Mead 1942: 14, 191).

When the child is learning to walk and to acquire other motor habits, the movements and gestures are performed with the teacher behind the pupil mechanically manipulating the pupil's limbs. Few words are spoken. To learn in such a manner the child must be relaxed and 'waxy limp' in the teacher's hands, with his consciousness almost in abeyance. The child learns to use his body by a direct sensori-kinesthetic rather than acoustic or ideational method. The teacher manipulates the flexible body of the pupil, always from behind, then leaves him to continue the pattern which has been impressed upon him (Gill and Brenman 1959: 301-302).

In initiation to the possession cult among the Songhay, the novice's old personality is supposed to be gone and the new god-personality has not yet been fixed, so that there is no personality present in his body. This is the passive, almost unconscious, tabula rasa state spoken of in the preceding chapter. In teaching the dance steps, a devotee stands in front of the novice, his toe touching that of the novice who passively follows the movements of the devotee's feet until the dance patterns become mechanical. The novice then performs alone (Rouch 1960).

Bateson and Mead state that the Balinese propensity for learning motor habits from watching others perform comes directly from their practice of learning passively as children, as has been outlined. Thus the child trance dancers are not taught their steps, but can supposedly dance because they are possessed by a god, and it is the god who is dancing. These little dancers frequently add new steps to their repertoire after seeing non-trance child dancers who have been taught their steps (1942: 15). The trance dancers have obviously picked up their steps from seeing, in their normal state, other dancers perform them. The Balinese, according to Bateson and Mead, learn virtually nothing from verbal instructions. Words must be assimilated into gestures to have any meaning for action.

The second striking characteristic of the Balinese image, related to the surrender of voluntary control, is the loose ego boundary. An important element in hypnosis is the fluidity and extensibility of body ego boundaries. Loosening of these boundaries is both a factor in inducing hypnosis and a phenomenon of the hypnotic state. In Bali, the body ego boundaries can easily be extended to include something in the external environment. A child, for example, will treat a plaything as an extension of his own body. Also a child is carried as if he were an appendage of the carrier's body which requires no special attention (Gill and Brenman 1959: 303-309).

This seems quite reasonable and commensurate with the fact that their perception of action is not intellectual but kinesthetic, so that they perceive action by physically identifying with it. This is like the good dancer who needs only to get the feel, physical and emotional, of a dance for the technical gestures to come easily and naturally. He translates his visual perceptions directly into corporal sensations and motor activity, with no intervening step of intellectualization.

Most learning in Bali thus seems to depend upon some measure of kinesthetic identification (Bateson and Mead 1942: 16). From the point of view of the teacher the child becomes an extension of the adult's ego boundary, but the adult likewise becomes an extension of the ego boundary of the child (Gill and Brenman 1959: 304, 307). There is a blending of teacher and taught, model and copyist (Bateson and Mead 1942: 17).

Such identification and mutual interpenetration of ego boundaries is analogous to the subject-hypnotist relationship. The subject becomes childlike and submissive, but since he incorporates the hypnotist as part of himself, he also participates in the latter's omnipotence. The hypnotist is not only omnipotent and directive, but also participates vicariously in the regression and passivity of the subject. The Balinese in a trance is both compliant and willful, and the crowd both subservient and completely in control of the subject's trance. The audience both looks on and participates. Spectators may fix a dancer's costume, suggest action, or join in madly chasing the Witch in the Witch and Dragon play (Gill and Brenman 1959: 306-307).

Bateson and Mead assert that the sense of personal uniqueness in Bali is slight. People are shy about mentioning their own or each other's names, yet each has an impersonal individuality which is tough and incontrovertible (1942: 45). Of course they could be hesitant to mention names for some reason totally unrelated to any sense of personal uniqueness or lack of same. The authors' statement sounds contradictory, but I imagine they mean that each person, of course, inevitably manifests individuality in his behavior, but that the Balinese are not very concerned with this individuality on a cognitive level. This fact seems commensurate with their ability to kinesthetically identify with the motor behavior of others.

Actually the socialization process, encouraging as it does both unresponsiveness and ego boundaries that may be extended to include those of others or merge with them, hardly seems propitious to the inculcation of much sense of personal uniqueness. The necessity of conforming to strict rules of decorum which dictate the types of attitudes to be shown on specific occasions, strictly prohibiting the expression of individual emotion, would reinforce this tendency to depersonalization. Interpersonal relations can not be very personal if no one may show how he really feels. Margaret Mead found that she had to adopt a very artificial, theatrical way of behaving to establish rapport with the Balinese.

In correlation with this lack of sense of personal uniqueness, we find that the complex Balinese religious system consists of a large pantheon of impersonal deities. This pantheon merges indistinguishably with the cult of the ancestors and with cults of village gods (Bateson and Mead 1942: 259). This impersonal pantheon is very different from those of the African and Afro-American pantheons being considered, in which each deity has a distinct personality and function known to all, which is assumed by the possessed devotee. In Bali, the mediums have specific deities who come to them in trances with advice for the people. The mediums may behave in a manner they think appropriate to their guiding deities, although the literature does not tell to what extent this is the case. People in different areas may also be possessed by the spirit of certain masks or animals, yet the majority of possessions do not seem to take on any individual character. The followers of the Witch and Dragon dance impersonally or run wildly around and stab themselves with krises (daggers), again with no personal distinction.[1] Perhaps their most impersonal trancelike manifestation is falling asleep in moments of anxiety, withdrawing all personal, individual expression.

Ease of trance induction in Bali is related to the fact that their primary autonomous and attention apparatuses already possess a relative degree of autonomy from their ordinary ego functioning, and can thus be readily recruited into a subsystem as previously discussed. Hence, trance induction in Bali probably requires less emphasis on de-automatization of bodily functions to upset the sense of bodily awareness, and more emphasis on the transference phenomenon (Gill and Brenman 1959: 309, 316-317). The Balinese seem to have some of the personality traits conducive to developing good transference relationships, such as strong need for dependence, repression as a dominant defense mechanism, and particularly great passivity.

In the village folk trances and the Witch and Dragon play there is no de-automatization. Both seem to involve auto-suggestion, although the Witch is ostensibly the hypnotist in the play. There is de-automatization for the child trance dancers. In all of these cases the transference relationship seems to be to the community of spectators, because they give suggestions, control the behavior of the trance subjects if it gets out of hand, and keep the trancers from

---

[1] Belo notes that the one person in a particular village who strove for individual self-expression and dramatic ostentation during his trances was different in character from most villagers, and not liked by them.

hurting themselves. The little girl trance dancers when inducted are smoked with incense like the mediums, and their bodies are shaken to promote de-automatization. When this happens they fall back limply against another person who supports them. They also depend upon the spectators for suggestions. Sometimes a little girl collapses into the audience, at which point she is set up by a spectator and begins to dance again almost automatically.

The theme of impersonation, role play, and disguise is prevalent in much of Haitian life, as exemplified in the impersonations of Carnival, the costuming of the Holy Week bands, and the theatrical performances of the raconteurs. Children as individuals or in groups like to pretend to be possessed by the Loa, and their elders encourage them in their play. Bourguignon gives an account of a little girl who played at being possessed for more than a week. With the encouragement of adults she kept returning to the same game, developing an alternate identity with corresponding patterns of activity. She learned to speak of herself in the third person, as people who have become gods do, and criticized her ordinary human behavior, as the incarnated Loa frequently do. She attempted to dissociate her identity as a little girl from that as a Loa, and to identify herself as the Loa with that same Loa as he mounted other people (1965: 48).

Such themes also appear frequently in Haitian Rorschachs. This is done in the form of distanciation, an indirect expression of psychological themes. When an unacceptable impulse is expressed in a response, it is more acceptable to the subject if he distinguishes between himself and the response by making the latter remote in time, space, person, or level of reality (Bourguignon 1965: 54). In the same vein, entranced Balinese report feeling as if they are in another place while in a trance, and back in place when they return to their normal state (Belo 1960: 224). Bateson and Mead (1942) report that the Balinese must know his exact location in time and space to feel that he is his normal self. In the distanciated trance state he is anything but his normal self and thus can express emotions and attitudes normally forbidden.

Such distanciation exists on an overt social level in the Zar cult. The Zar are so much a part of the life of cult members that they intervene constantly in everyday life. They may be called upon to justify activity, a mood, or a decision, or to assume responsibility for some activity of the devotee's for which the latter does not want to be held responsible. There seems to be an implicit understanding [seemingly unique to the Zar cult among the groups in question] tha it is not a mythical personality who is acting, but a human in a state other than the normal, yet not really as distinct as the change of name and supposed change of status seem to indicate (Leiris 1958: 67, 78). The Zar cult differs from the Haitian and other groups in recognizing that it is really one's self who is acting rather than a deity, yet it is the deity who is held responsible. The Ethiopians implicitly recognize a continuity of the basic personality which the other groups deny.

In Haiti, no continuity in self-identity is expected for the possessed person, although it is for his deity. There is not even physiological continuity in bodily responses because all such responses during possession are attributed to the deity not to the devotee. For example, a person made ill by alcohol in his normal state may be possessed by a deity who drinks freely with no ill effects at that time or upon returning to normal. A person so crippled by rheumatism he can hardly get around in normal life will dance with great agility while possessed, but in this case may understandably have subsequent ill effects (Bourguignon 1965: 47).

The belief in Zombis reflects this same belief in the loose connection of body and self. Zombis exemplify the continuity of part of the self, the body, in the absence of continuity of memory or the sense of identity, or even under circumstances of gross bodily alteration. [The Zombi has supposedly returned from the dead at the bidding of a priest.] There is more continuity of self in the Zombi state than in possession (Bourguignon 1965: 47). In possession even the body does not really continue in its normal form because the whole physiognomy and posture change to adapt to the personality and bearing of the deity. The Zombi is still the same person, though in a very different state, whereas the possessed person is no longer himself, but a god.

Another essential underlying theme related to the idea of the partial and loose connection of body and self, is that appearances may be deceptive. Things, people, and animals are often not what they appear. An animal may be a person, a snake may be the Loa Damballah, a person seen while awake or in a dream may be a Loa, and people may be Zombis (Bourguignon 1965: 47). I think that it would probably be more correct to say that the Haitians undoubtedly recognize and accept the fact that things are in a sense what they

appear to be, but are also something else, on a more significant
plane, and it is the latter meaning which takes precedence. This type
of outlook seems quite propitious to or consonant with a belief that
when people act in a manner different from their ordinary norm, it is
because they are no longer themselves but someone else. Of course
everyone knows who the possessed people are on an objective,
profane level, but what is important at the moment is that they have
become deities on the more important sacred, ritual plane.

Haitian children receive realistic toilet and sex training with co-
operation and understanding from adults, hence do not develop an
aggressive attitude toward their social environment at this period.
Underwood feels that this contributes to the friendliness and
openness of the Haitian peasants she studied. They have, however, a
low frustration level which is probably the result of both constant
hunger and a factor in the child rearing process (1947: 571-572).

As soon as children are verbally intelligible and physically coordinated they experience a radical variation in their social
environment. Before this point they were protected, indulged,
coddled, and given much attention. Suddenly their whims and desires
are restricted, attention to them becomes casual, and discipline from
elders becomes stern and oppressive. Training for adult roles begins,
and must be a rapid process because of the lack of adult time and the
need for added labor. The necessity for respect and obedience to all
elders is rapidly impressed upon the children. Since enforcement of
this educational process is in the hands of volatile individuals, the
atmosphere in which the child must learn is productive of insecurity
and emotional ambivalence (Underwood 1947: 572).

The Haitian adult personality structure is characterized by
extroversion and curiosity, volatility, relative aggressiveness, relative
individualism, and relative insecurity. Security is so strongly a
function of group activity that Underwood noted only a few instances
of solitary activity in her six week stay, and this by people who were
not average members of the community (Underwood 1947: 573).

Individuals are allowed considerable freedom of emotional
expression. This is the basis of their individuality but also produces
their volatility and excitability. Emotional outbursts come easily to
them. They laugh, cry, and get angry easily. Underwood attributes
this tendency to the radical change in child treatment. She considers
this change also responsible for their degree of insecurity and
aggressiveness. The latter may be dissipated in gossip, teasing, joking,

and magic. Mistreatment of wives and children is common (Underwood 1947: 574). Such aggressiveness may be directly expressed, and the insecurity compensated for, during possession.

As might be expected, there are ambivalent feelings toward authority figures in Haiti. The child is taught early by beatings and scoldings that all elders, including siblings, must be unquestioningly obeyed. The family (including the dead members), the Vodun cult group, the Loa, the Catholic church, the social structure — all are organized on the basis of a strict hierarchy of age and power. One exerts authority over one's inferiors and the power of superiors must be respected and obeyed. Superiors may be manipulated and placated, never opposed. Such a situation is bound to produce much aggression which can not be expressed openly. Aggression may be displaced to evil spirits, and in possession one may express such aggression toward superiors in culturally sanctioned form (Bourguignon 1959: 43-44). There are certain Loa, usually peasant prototypes, whose main function is to tell the rich and powerful what the poor peasants really think of them. Although under normal circumstances faking possession is highly disapproved, it is permissible when a person does so in order to speak his mind to a superior.

Wittkower describes the possession state as a phenomenon of suggestion in a suggestible person living in a culture which fosters submissiveness and hence suggestibility. The more suggestible a person is the more likely he is to pass into a possession state (1964: 79). His is, of course, not a total explanation of possession, but it is pertinent. The Haitian way of life entails complete submission to one's superiors and to the will of the gods. The same emphasis on submissiveness is characteristic of the childrearing process in which children are forced to obey and curb their feelings of aggression toward their elders by corporal punishment and threats of harm from the werewolves and other evil spirits with which the environment is populated.

In addition, the rural Haitian child is exposed to ceremonial possession from an early age. He is aware of the prestige of the houngan and the possessed people, and he learns of their good fortune. Thus he hopes that when he grows up he also will have a possessing Loa. He will serve his Loa by dancing for him, and in return he will have a guardian spirit who will protect him and on whom he can call in time of trouble. Such beliefs evidently increase his sense of security.

The stimulus-frustration pattern in Balinese child rearing can be seen as analogous, in some senses, to the radical indulgence-discipline transition in Haitian socialization. In Bali this pattern prepares the individual for the culturally prescribed behavior of observing strict decorum and not expressing personal emotions in a normal state. The Haitians do express personal emotions to their peers and inferiors, but never to superiors, having learned this lesson under some duress. Also the Haitian peasants live in a situation in which they are aware of their superiors. They must feel envy and pent-up aggressiveness toward the people who live in luxury, as compared to their abject poverty. Neither their desire to occupy such a position, nor their feelings of aggression can be manifest in a normal situation. The trance in Bali and Haitian possession by the Loa permit the culturally sanctioned expression of such normally prohibited impulses.

It is commensurate with the Balinese unresponsiveness and impersonal quality that in trances they do not manifest specific individual personalities expressing different emotional tones. Some Balinese, particularly the kris dancers, reported to Belo feeling what they described as 'angry, overcome, crazy', while in the trance state. This is Balinese phrasing for the storm of strong emotion showing itself in the convulsive fits which end many trances. They do not remember any other affect. It is significant that anger is not an emotion which is customarily expressed in the normal state. People appear to swallow their resentment or express it indirectly by having a spell cast on an enemy, or in extreme cases they let it burst out after a long period of brooding in an attack of violent running amok. Hence the trance seems to provide a culturally sanctioned opportunity to express pent-up, repressed anger (Belo 1960: 223-224). This sounds quite reasonable given that the prime emotions built up by the frustrations of childhood are probably anger and hostility.

In Haiti on the other hand, the peasants are individualistic and emotional, as reflected in the individualism and dynamic quality of the personalities of their deities. In most cases the characteristics of one's deity correspond to elements of one's personality which can not ordinarily be expressed for one reason or another. Also the Haitian peasants, being at the bottom of the social scale, probably feel the need to assert themselves rather than to be submissive, yet they can not do so ordinarily because of their social position and because they have not been inculcated with such personality characteristics. Also, being in contact with more affluent people probably feeds their fantasy life so that they fulfill their fantasies by taking on roles in possession which they would like to play in real life.

Balinese trances do not seem to include this component of wish fulfillment role playing. Entranced people may become the Witch or Dragon or one of their followers, or a zoomorphic mask, or an animal, but they do not seem to assume any role they would like to play in real life. The Balinese seem to be very much lacking in spontaneity, even in their trances, as evidenced by their stereotyped behavior and emotion, which would follow from the emphasis on decorum, not expressing emotions, and perceiving more identity than differences between people. The Haitians, on the contrary, add individual and spontaneous touches to the basic personalities of their deities. The entranced Balinese appears to experience extreme, amorphous feelings, whereas the Haitian becomes an entirely different person with a new personality, physiognomy, type of behavior, status, and life style. That the Balinese trance is allowed to become much more anarchistic than that in Haiti (and the other groups in question) is perhaps related to this fundamental lack of structure in prescribed trance self-expression, as well as to the fact that such severely repressed emotions probably demand violent release. The degree of anarchy in trance manifestations is probably inversely proportional in some degree to the normal amount of emotional expression in everyday life.

Thus by looking at the phenomenon and institution of trance and possession in various socio-cultural settings from the perspective of the type of personality inculcated by the child socialization process, one can note the radically different content with which the same form may be filled in different societies. Since the child socialization process is designed to form personality types suited to the demands of the society, observance of the content of the possession phenomenon can indicate a great deal about the basic values, attitudes, and ways of being of the community. The Balinese, with little sense of personal identity, behave and apparently feel the same way in possession. The majority of trancers are not possessed by deities at all, and there are apparently no guardian spirits an individual may invoke. Being entranced does not seem to have the prestige possession has in Haiti, so the main incentive seems to be the opportunity to express pent-up emotion in socially approved form and to participate in an enjoyable community ceremony. The

Balinese do not have the complete secondary personality subsystems that the Haitians manifest in possession. They seem merely to express explosions of personal affect in a very generalized, impersonal manner.

A final difference may be observed in their contrasting reactions to situations of stress. The Balinese passively withdraw. They do not deal with the situation at all, but go to sleep. If they can not escape they behave irrationally. The Haitians, in contrast, deal with such situations beyond their normal capacity by summoning their guardian Loa. In becoming possessed by the Loa, or activating a subsystem of their personalities, they can now deal actively and efficiently with the situation.

Gill and Brenman suggest that trance manifestations in different societies may vary in whether they are chiefly dominated by the id or by the environment after ego autonomy is lost (1959: 318). The Balinese seem to exhibit both tendencies in different types of trance. The folk trancers and little girl trance dancers seem to be dominated by the environment because they respond very much to the suggestions of the spectators. The members of the Witch and Dragon play, those trancers who experience so much anger, are apparently dominated by the id.

In Haiti and the other areas there is less of an either-or situation. Most people's possessions are dominated by both id and environment at the same time in the form of the compromise formation ego subsystem which is the god's personality. The id impulses are expressed within a cultural pattern chosen to harmonize with the devotee's own personal tendencies. In some individuals one or the other possibility may take the lead. The possessed person may just be playing a culturally prescribed role that does not necessarily correspond to his psychological needs. Or, in some societies cultural control is or is becoming so lax that the individual merely acts out his desires and impulses in an idiosyncratic manner. Of course the content of these idiosyncratic fantasies is derived from the individual's culture, but the fantasies are idiosyncratic because they are not fitted into a culturally approved pattern.

Consideration of the relationship between these socialization processes and corresponding religious projective systems has led me to reconsider Spiro and D'Andrade's proposition that the character of the supernatural beings in a society is a projection of the parent imago as seen from the child's point of view during early socialization (1958: 457). This theory is perhaps valid when people relate to their deities from a distance, but it does not seem to hold true for the religions in question, where people actually become their deities. In Bali the gods are seen and treated as children, and in the other areas they are mostly adults with attributes corresponding to the fantasies of the devotees. The only similarity to the parent imago is that the gods are omnipotent and omniscient, and must be obeyed. They also may be irrational as parents often seem. These, however, are rather general attributes of deities and parents, and the formulation accounts for nothing significant in the consideration of the character of the supernatural in the societies in question.

I contend that in religions in which one is possessed by the deities, and thus assumes their attributes, the character of the deities is either a re-enactment of the stage of life most enjoyed, or a projection of what one would like to be in life. In Bali people in trances behave like little children. They cry, call out to their fathers and mothers, and express urgent and unpredictable desires about which they will not be quieted until satisfied. Being like gods they behave like children (Belo 1960: 13). The gods are seen as children and very young children as gods. The ideal personification of the gods is in the person of the little girl trance dancers. These little girls, normally too old to be indulged like babies, are endowed with power and sanctity by the crowd in their entranced state. They are gods for the moment and are pampered like babies. The audience finds their peevishness amusing unless they go too far, in which case the audience loses patience (Belo 1960: 4, 185, 189). The gods are thought of as children of the people, not august parental figures. Speaking through mediums they address villagers as mother and father (Bateson and Mead 1942: 29). Hence we see that the supernatural image in Bali is a projection of the time of greatest comfort and security—infancy. The trancers try to return to this stage of life when they were treated best, and when they were considered gods.[1] The parental image in Bali is projected into the theater in the Witch and Dragon plays.

---

[1] In some villages Balinese folk trance dancers become common animals such as dogs and pigs or common household objects such as brooms. Those who become animals report experiencing delicious feelings and thoughts, and being very pleased to do whatever the animal does, such as play and romp until it has had enough, or wallow in the mud (Belo 1960: 222). Such behavior is not at all in harmony with Balinese norms, yet is apparently very enjoyable to both participants and to spectators vicariously under trance conditions.

In Brazil, Trinidad, and Yorubaland, but not in Haiti or the other African and Afro-American areas, there is frequently a transition period going in and out of possession known as éré, wéré, or réré. Éré is considered either a stage of semi-possession or possession by a helper of one of the deities. It is characterized by childish gaiety (Simpson 1962: 1211). This childish, regressive behavior is still directly pleasurable to the individual and may have symbolic meanings. It is probably a re-enactment of behavior which is still gratifying (Mischel and Mischel 1958: 253). In Haiti this stage does not exist but most of the gods like to sing and dance and have a good time. People are tolerant and indulgent with them if they cause a disorder as they are with young children (Deren 1953: 123). Hence possession is like hypnosis in its regressive revival of earlier parent-child relationships. The gods have authority like parents but the people's attitude toward them combines respect with banter, treating them as both superiors and peers. This is, of course, exactly what they are since they are both gods and themselves. Thus in possession the devotee is both omnipotent as the god, and submissive as himself. He can dominate the spectators but also depend upon them, so he is at the same time an omnipotent parent with a gratifying life style, and a pampered child.

CHAPTER FIVE

POSSESSION AND CULTURAL DETERMINISM

The enormous importance of the element of cultural determinism in the realm of possession and hallucination is clearly illustrated in an example of clinical research with hallucinogenic compounds. In these experiments subjects are given the drug and asked to report verbally on their subjective experiences. Their responses vary greatly depending upon their own attitudes toward the distortion of their normal sensory and cognitive experience, therefore can not be assumed to indicate a determined physiological effect of the drugs (Wallace 1959: 63). Although individual attitudes will, of course, vary within any society, a certain basic orientation will be provided by the culture.

The following is a comparison of the responses of American whites and habitually peyote-taking Indians to a clinical experiment involving the taking of peyote (Wallace 1959: 63). The element of cultural determinism is blatant, the differences in white and Indian responses being so vast as to appear related to totally different phenomena — which they actually are in psycho-cultural though not in physiological terms.

Whites	Indians
Varied and extreme mood shifts — agitated depression, anxiety, euphoria, depending upon stage of intoxication and personal characteristics.	Initial relative stability of mood followed by religious enthusiasm and anxiety, with a tendency toward feelings of religious reverence and personal satisfaction when a vision was achieved, and often expectations of relief from physical illness.
Free breakdown of social inhibitions and display of 'shameless' sexual, aggressive, etc. behavior.	Maintenance of orderly and 'proper' behavior — revivalistic enthusiasm socially proper in this context.
All subjects suspicious of others present in environment. This reported by observers and noted in self.	No report of suspiciousness,
Unwelcome feelings of loss of contact with reality, depersonaliza-	*Welcome* feelings of contact with a new, more meaningful, higher order

tion, meaninglessness, 'split' personality, etc.

of reality, but a reality prefigured in
their doctrinal knowledge, and
implying more, rather than less,
social participation.

Hallucinations largely idiosyncratic
in content.

Hallucinations often strongly patterned after doctrinal models.

No therapeutic benefits or permanent change.

Marked therapeutic benefits and
behavioral changes — reduction of
chronic anxiety level, increased
sense of personal worth, more
satisfaction in community life.

The non-physiological reasons for the differences in response are
related to the setting in which the drugs are normally taken, and the
different psycho-cultural meanings of the experience of the primary
effects of the drugs (Wallace 1959: 64). It was also noted in clinical
experiments with photic driving that the variety in evoked response
and most of the characteristic abnormalities were the result not of the
elementary physiological effects, but of indirect or secondary factors
including such features as physical condition, psychological make-up,
and cultural values (Walter and Grey 1949: 63). The whites, according
to Wallace, take peyote infrequently, and only in a clinical setting,
are aware of the experimental purpose of the act, and have no
commitment to the taking of peyote as a personal religious
sacrament. The Indians take peyote as a sacrament in a ceremonial
lodge during a solemn religious ritual. They have a definite purpose
for its usage and often hope for personal salvation, of which the
resultant visions are evidence (1959: 64).

For the whites, there are no systematized cultural determinants of
the behavior to be induced by the taking of peyote except some
attitudes which in general militate against losing one's rational
orientation in a situation of cognitive and perceptual disorientation.
The result is an extreme disorientation and instability that may very
well represent an unconscious desire to get rid of all control to the
point of total chaos. The Indians experience, in a very personal way,
communion with their supernatural world, and their reactions are
more structured than those of the whites because their experiences
follow structured, positively evaluated, culturally determined demand
characteristics. The whites are behaving according to the demand
characteristics which they perceive to be involved in the peyote

experience. However, their culture generally disapproves of such altered states of consciousness, and therefore provides no framework to direct their behavior. Thus their behavior is characterized by confusion, discomfort, and lack of normal self-control. It is interesting to note that the Indians' reactions to peyote are very similar to the reactions of the possessed people in the African and New World African religions in consideration. The reactions of the whites appear rather 'hysterical', which gives some indication as to why early researchers considered possession a hysterical manifestation.

Wallace's example calls attention to the fact that cultural determinants can produce very different psychological and behavioral results built upon the same common physiological substratum. It has been established that states neurophysiologically, psychologically and behaviorally similar to possession can be induced by sonic driving or hypnosis, but although the form may be the same, the content is largely dependent upon cultural factors.

Possessed individuals express usually concealed personal tendencies but always follow strict cultural dictates in the still well-organized cults. Ceremonial possession is a result of social pressure on the individual. It begins and ends at the proper time and obeys set rules. Deities who come when they are not wanted are sent away. In Bahia the possessed individuals are reliving the lives and acts of the Orisha and hence must follow the traditional order of procedure.

The individual has learned during initiation to channel his idiosyncratic tendencies into culturally valued patterns, and to manifest these imposed patterns on cue. Verger stresses the important fact that the devotee becomes possessed only when he hears the rhythm of his own deity (1954: 328). If the mystical seizure were merely the effect of the sonic driving of the drums, with the added impetus of the ceremonial atmosphere, bodies packed together, and the fatigue of dancing, there is no reason for which the possession should not come at any moment in the ceremony. That it awaits a specific rhythmic cue indicates the essential role of the cultural element which influences what otherwise appears to be a purely neurophysiological reaction.

In Dutch Guiana and Dahomey the devotees fear hearing their rhythms because they are afraid that they will begin to dance and never be able to stop. In Bahia and Haiti, however, it is possible to remain completely calm while hearing, under different circumstances, the same rhythms that normally lead to possession. The same rhythms at a funeral or a social event do not produce possession as they do in religious ceremonies. Women in mourning in Haiti are not supposed to be possessed. They can attend religious ceremonies and listen, with no effect, to the music of their own gods to which normally they would respond by becoming possessed. Also in the Candomblé social dances the same possession-invoking rhythms are played, but on unbaptized drums. No possession ensues (Bastide 1953: 45-46).

Despite the possibility of incipient purely neurophysiological responses to the drums, the element of cultural approval is necessary for actual possession to take place. In the situations in which one is to remain calm, the expectation of remaining so evidently works to counteract the effect of the drums. According to Verger, if the ensemble of factors, such as herbal baths and observance of taboos, are not brought together at the right time and place, the drum rhythms alone will have no effect on the Bahians (1954: 328). It is apparent that in the areas in which a devotee is afraid to hear the deity's songs and rhythms, hearing such rhythms without any other factors, is sufficient to bring the deity on. This is equally the result of cultural determinism since it is only one's own, and not just any similar rhythm, which will suffice, although the frequency of the drum rhythm may be the same, and thus should have the same neurophysiological effect.

Even some factors which one would expect to be controlled by the possessed individual are culturally determined. According to Bastide, the violence of possession depends more upon the character of the mythical model than on the person's own tendencies. Ogun, god of war, provides a violent possession in contrast with Oshun, goddess of fresh water, whose possession is quite mild and agreeable (1960: 521). I would say rather that the violence of the possession is more a result of the interaction between the character of the god, the temperament of the individual, and particular circumstances of the moment. Also the person's deity is chosen in most cases in harmony with something in his personality so the violence or lack of it in the god's manifestation would be related to the person's personality. The possessed person is harnessed by the injunction to dance to the drums. He is forbidden to eat, drink, or satisfy other wants. Landes never saw anyone scratch, yawn, stretch, or relieve his biological needs during a twelve hour period (1947: 54). The possessed respond only to the signals of the priest or priestess and the drums.

In the Zar cult there is a certain season during which most possessions take place. It is the season of abundance during which there is little work to be done, which indicates something about the institutionalized nature of possession and its link with social life. (Leiris 1958: 32). An Ethiopian from Gondar told me that it was customary for pretty young girls to become possessed in the market place on Saint John's Day. In Brazil the Orisha are sent away during Lent and do not even come on non-ceremonial occasions to give warnings or messages to their devotees. The same is true among the Songhay during Ramadan.

The ceremonial situation increases the possibility of possession for most people present, but it can also be equally influential in the opposite direction for those people who can not desert vital ceremonial tasks. Sentiments and sanctions create a different social reality for the priest, drummers, and other officers (Ravenscroft 1965: 178). These individuals may be capable of possession at other times, but when they are functioning in ceremonies the psychological conditions and social pressure preclude this eventuality. Actually this is not consistently true in all of the cults but is true in the traditional Brazilian and possibly in the African cults. In Haiti the houngan is sometimes possessed while presiding. He is, however, usually very much in control of the situation. The drummers often seem to be in a light trance although they may not actually become possessed. Herskovits cites instances in Trinidad in which a drummer suddenly surrenders his drum to another and becomes possessed.

In Dahomey a person who is away from his own cult group but near another must avoid hearing the music unless he asks the priest in charge if he may borrow a costume and dance. In Haiti only members of the family are to be possessed at family ceremonies whereas anyone can be possessed at public ceremonies. Members of the Candomblé consider it in very bad form for anyone who is not a member of the particular community group to allow himself to be possessed at a ceremony other than that of his own group. Visitors to the Candomblé who feel themselves becoming possessed will drink cold water, of which the Orisha are afraid, to calm themselves. All of these features exemplify the degree to which possession is controlled by the community.

There are limits to the freedom the individual has in inserting his own personality into the pattern furnished by the god. Exploitation beyond social bounds of the role and license of the gods is one of the most highly tabooed acts, and unleashes fierce social control against 'false gods' (Ravenscroft 1965: 169).

Bastide suggests that some of the godly roles that people play when possessed are just imposed by the society and do not respond to any psychological needs of the individual. The devotees are merely playing dramatic roles imposed from without (1950: 252). This is most likely the case in traditional Dahomey where an individual is chosen by his family to serve a god, with little or no thought as to how the god's personality coincides with that of the chosen devotee. Of course these are the people who have the most rigorous initiation period at the end of which the god is perhaps very much a part of their personalities. People get more or less deeply into their roles depending upon a number of personality factors such as the ability to identify with the role because of what it corresponds to in their own personalities, the appeal the designated personality type presents to them, plus their ability to forget themselves and become someone else. The African and Afro-American groups exemplify the former tendencies and the Balinese seem to have a particular propensity for the latter.

It would seem reasonable that the possession phenomenon, since it is so well planned, would permit a good deal of what Bastide terms 'sociological possession', but I think that it is a matter of degree rather than absolutes. Possession obviously corresponds to a desire to dress up, play act, be the center of attention, and gain prestige, all very important psychologically. Herskovits questions whether the rigid patterning of ceremonial possession in Dahomey, by checking the individual's manifestations, does not diminish the individual ecstasy that might be expected from the awareness of having a Vodun within oneself. Dahomean skeptics say the individual gets out of possession nothing but the enjoyment of being free from routine tasks, and the pleasure of appearing before friends in cult finery. Women enjoy the status and the favorable position the family must accord them.[1] Some feel a oneness with the Vodun, a sense of awe

---

[1] Most Dahomean men would rather their wives not become devotees of the Voduns because they will no longer be able to control them. They can not, however, stand in the way of determined wives. The Ethiopian who had seen the Zar-possessed women in Gondar said that he would not want his wife to have a Zar because a woman with a Zar can make too many demands on her husband which he must fulfill or the Zar will take his wife away. Of course many women pretend to be possessed by the Zar to make demands of their husbands.

and exaltation, and the emotion held in check between ceremonies is brought into play during actual possession (1933: 48).

Hence cultural determinism is the most important feature in patterning the content of the possession phenomenon, the substrata of which can be explained in purely neurophysiological and psychological terms as a hypnotoform state. Even the features that seem to be purely physiological in nature respond to this cultural patterning. The personality of each god has the same substratum but because of cultural determinism these deities are perceived and manifest with amazing variety. It is difficult to distinguish exactly what the degree of neurophysiological influence is, since the cultural element obviously plays so great a role.

CHAPTER SIX

POSSESSION AND THE INDIVIDUAL

A significant correlation can be seen between individual development and spirit possession. My specific data is from Haiti but the same principle can be applied to the other areas, excluding Bali, with some modifications. In Haiti girls marry and assume adult responsibilities and functions between the ages of seventeen and twenty-two, men between twenty-two and twenty-eight. The first possession usually comes in this period when the individual begins to assume responsibilities and suffer the stresses of the society. Possessions decline and cease between the ages of forty-five and sixty. This is the period when people become physically and socially dependent upon their children, who serve them with due respect (Ravenscroft 1965: 174). Also with age and experience people obtain more spiritual control over the gods by feeding them and gaining esoteric knowledge. They are more rarely possessed and like to think of themselves as mastering, rather than serving, the deities (Bourguignon 1965: 49; Landes 1940: 53-54).

In Haiti an estimated thirty per cent of initial possessions occur outside of the ceremonial atmosphere (Ravenscroft 1965: 180). This is striking because the devotee has not experienced the ceremonial possession which would seem to facilitate subsequent occurrences. Since the first possession is the most difficult, the private circumstances arousing the individual are crucial because the external reality provides less than optimum cues. Common personal circumstances often existing in temporal proximity to the first possession are the death or estrangement of an important family member, or an important change in the peasant's social status or personal responsibility, which may follow from the former factor. The actual possession may occur under the most ordinary of circumstances, when the individual may or may not be thinking of anything pertaining directly to Vodun (Ravenscroft 1965: 180). The change in life circumstances probably precipitates the onset of the first possession by causing a build-up of stress and tension.

An individual's first ceremonial possession is by an unsocialized deity, in Haiti a 'Loa bossal', and in Bahia a 'santo bruto', which means that the person's behavior does not conform to that of any specific deity, and is usually quite uncontrolled. The identity of this deity must be ascertained by the priests, and the new devotee must be initiated or taught how to control his possession by fitting his behavior into the patterns of the deity's personality.

Haitian non-ceremonial initial possession appears similar to the initial indications among the Zar cult members and the Songhay that a deity wants a person as his devotee. The individual may become withdrawn and/or hysterical in alternating spells. The identity of the deity must be ascertained and the individual taught to serve him in possession. The first sign is not, then, real possession, but rather personal impulses and desires struggling for expression in yet inchoate form. What these desires and impulses are becomes clear in the deity chosen. His personality traits correspond, in socialized form, to what the individual is trying to express.

Awareness of the pantheon of possessing deities is not limited to ceremonial situations. It is an integral and all-pervasive part of each individual's perception of reality. The gods are always present, associated with natural features and events, and they intervene in daily life. They are omnipotent, omniscient, and omnipresent. In Haiti, as has been indicated, people are sometimes possessed by their gods in times of stress. Bourguignon (1965) reports that the Loa can also be invoked for brief periods on non-ritual occasions for purely personal reasons. The reason in the instance cited was to please the field worker. She does not mention whether the woman in question was a priestess and therefore more able to invoke deities at will than the average devotee. This woman consciously and in a controlled manner desired possession by Ogun. When he left, Guédé came unbidden to retort to Ogun's aspersions against him. The deities were both manifestly aware of the presence of a neighbor and the anthropologist.

The Holey play an important role in the everyday life of the Songhay. They may, for example, be attributed with saving someone from drowning, myth and reality being one and the same (Rouch 1960: 81). Likewise, the Zar may be seen as the heroes of certain human events of which they are placed at the origin. These events are then integrated into the specific Zar's own myths (Leiris 1958: 67). Zar also intervene constantly in everyday affairs. They may interfere in domestic affairs, like by preventing marriages. Women often get possessed if their husbands beat them or if they are unhappy about their marital situation (Leiris 1958: 64). Among the

Taita of Kenya, women may become possessed specifically to force their husbands to accede to their wishes (Harris 1957).

Some Zar are linked to certain specific circumstances and appear to be automatically invoked by them. Such instances may be the construction or repair of a house, angry disputes, healing, etc. On such occasions the individual assumes the identity and behavior of the appropriate Zar (Leiris 1958: 64). This is analogous to the phenomenon of spontaneous possession in Haiti. As already stated, the individual can cope with situations beyond his normal competence by temporarily becoming his deity.

Purely private acts of an individual may be attributed to the Zar because they are more in keeping with the latter's character than with that of the former. Changes occurring in the character or habitual conduct of a person are usually attributed to his Zar. Since the Zar are seen as constantly intervening in life, people treat them as responsible when they feel the need, vis-à-vis themselves or others, to justify, explain, or excuse conduct, or give weight to a decision, declaration, or act, which is then seen as emanating from a very powerful source (Leiris 1958: 70-73). Through these possessing deities, therefore, one can explain all of reality — illness and death, changes in character, good and bad luck, and apparently chance events also. Everything can be known.

The extent of an individual's participation in the possession phenomenon depends upon his personality traits, the amount of interest his family has in the cult, and the turns his fortune takes (Simpson 1945: 54). Some people may be or pretend to be possessed mainly for the attention it brings to them. A person who has no serious difficulties in the course of life may never be called upon to ask whether or not he is properly serving his gods. He may never be placed in a situation in which possession would be necessary as a release (Herskovits 1966: 359).

The devotee must surrender his own ego for the godly archetype to become manifest in him. Maya Deren sees this as painful self-sacrifice for the sake of spectators, since the individual does not even remember what he has done (1953: 249). Rodolphe Derose, one of the Haitian évolués who sees Vodun as a satanic primitive evil, feels that serving and becoming possessed by the gods removes from man his principle attribute, the right to dispose of himself. He feels that it destroys his psychological autonomy and creates diminished human beings with limited liberty and fields of action (1956: viii-iv).

Both authors seem to show a great lack of understanding of the mechanisms of the religion. For serving the gods one receives in payment a sense of security and in possession one may live one's desires and fantasies. The surrender of the normal ego functions is not self-sacrifice, but rather the door to greater freedom. Far from losing one's autonomy and field of action, both possession and the sense of security engendered by serving the gods much increase such capacities. The possessed individuals are actualizing themselves on a plane of reality more powerful, sacred, and meaningful than the everyday.

The repertoire of deity personalities is large, and the behavior patterns are vague and flexible enough to allow much individual variation and innovation. Each deity's manifestation varies from devotee to devotee in tastes, activities, demands, tractability, etc. In all but the most traditional areas new deities may make their appearance by announcing themselves to their servants-to-be in dreams or in spontaneous ceremonial possession. Thus the non-traditional pantheon is in a constant state of flux and modification, although the central deities remain constant. The individual's field of action is thus broadened because ritual possession provides an alternate set of roles in which desires, unrealistic in the real world, may be fulfilled in the most concrete manner possible. Such dramatic enactment is much more real than playing different roles in the theater because it is lived rather than played. The participants consider the events of the ritual drama as real as or more real than the events of the everyday world. The audience is not skeptical, dispassionate, and incredulous. In such a world of poverty, disease, and frustration as exists in most of the areas under consideration, ritual possession, rather than destroying the integrity of the self, provides an increased scope for fulfillment (Bourguignon 1965: 49, 57).

For example, a mild-mannered Haitian, usually ignored and pushed around by his kin, is possessed by one of the most powerful deities in his family. When he is possessed his family pays him great deference, and his possessions seem to last longer than most. A dim-witted man's principal deity is crucial to an annual ritual. Without him his brother, a successful houngan, can not conduct the ceremony (Bourguignon 1965: 53, 57). Since it seems that even in areas where there is supposedly no identification of the devotee with his deity, such identification is tacitly recognized in everyday behavior patterns, it follows that the importance one gains from very close ties with a deity carries over into everyday life.

Belo noticed that aged or unattractive, humble, mousy Balinese women often went into very abandoned trances, surprising in their violence and in the completeness with which they gave themselves up to the trance. They were apparently compensating for an urgent need which their lives created in them. They were forgetful in their conduct and more exhibitionist than more attractive girls because they were denied the appreciation of their beauty that many women tend to expect. After the preliminary ritual had gone on for hours, mousy women seemed to come from nowhere and hurl themselves into the middle of the action at the height of the trance. Their trance behavior had an astonishingly ferocious urgency and they had probably been present at the preliminaries but kept out of sight until the height of the trance came, at which point they jumped into the activity with a vengeance (Belo 1960: 157).

According to Leiris, the Zar cult offers the individual a repertoire of personalities to be taken according to the necessities and various hazards of daily life. These personalities, which offer ready-made attitudes and behavior, are halfway between real life and the theater. Leiris noticed that a respected Zar cult leader was possessed by numerous different Zar, a particular one for each daily activity, e.g., one for serving ritual coffee as a cure, one for giving her entourage moral counsel, another for business deals, and still another when she supervised the obtaining of animals for sacrifice (1958: 7-8). As in Haiti, there is probably a hierarchy of possession probabilities. In Haiti the average number of deities per person is three, although a person may have as many as sixty deities by whom he is possessed fairly regularly at appropriate times (Ravenscroft 1965: 171). This latter situation is most likely very exceptional.

> The religious community furnishes the individual with a certain number of well-known consecrated models of divinities characterized by certain libidinous attitudes, through which his conflicts may express themselves instead of developing into neuropathic symptoms, and even acquire a useful function for the group since they become ways to better represent mythical history. There is a synthesis of the collective representations imposed by the ancestral religion and individual unconscious tendencies, so that the latter are put into an historic sequence controlled by tradition, subject to a development which takes from them all harmful force, dulls their dangerous points (Bastide 1950: 252 — author's translation).

In the aesthetically satisfying atmosphere of joy and festivities, suppressed and repressed aspects of the personality come to the fore in symbolic, socially approved form. This is an important element in maintaining both social and individual equilibrium. In possession the individual may free himself of conflicts, complexes, and hidden tendencies in dancing for the god whose characteristics are in some way analogous to his own. Instead of the seemingly flat and incomplete technique of trying to express one's unconscious self only verbally while lying on an analyst's couch isolated from society, the possessed individual expresses himself with his whole body through drama and dance in a situation involving many of the people with whom he normally interacts.

It seems evident to me (and I was pleased to note that Bastide (1950: 252) also mentions the fact) that possession is a prototypical form of Jacob Moreno's psychodrama, a psychotherapeutic technique characterized by the individual's working out of his problems in dramatic interaction with other people who play the roles of significant others in his life. These possession rituals can be more precisely termed hypno-sociodramas, because the participants are in a hypnotoform state and their behavior must exhibit elements of social interaction typical of their community.

Louis Mars refers to ceremonial possession as 'ethnodrama' which it is in two senses (1966). In acting out the characters of the gods the participants are recreating the mythical history of their society. They are also, however, reflecting the actual social history and present realities of the community. It would seem that present social issues and tensions must come to the surface in such ceremonies. Perhaps acting them out openly and reacting to them in a ceremonial context helps the society to function more smoothly.

In Haiti, for example, the characteristics of the gods are revealing of the class structure. Ogun is powerful, domineering, drinks rum, and speaks French like a 'gros nègre'. Guédé, in contrast, is lower class, parodies upper class pretentions, and may insult and demean any upper class or upwardly aspiring people present. He drinks clairin (cheap rum), eats lowly food, speaks Creole, lives in the cemetery, represents the dead, and is both obscene and associated with fertility and birth. Erzulie, goddess of love, is light-skinned with straight hair, likes expensive clothing, jewelry, and perfume, speaks French, and flirts with all of the male Loa except the lowly Guédé. Zaca, the peasant, is called cousin rather than papa like the other

Loa, wears a peasant costume,   and is ignorant of city ways (Bourguignon 1965: 52). The individual expresses his social aspirations and/or attitudes by whichever god he becomes. The Loa's interaction with other Loa and with the spectators is indicative of the social climate.

On a more individual level possession seems to me to be clearly a form of hypnodrama. This is a form of psychodrama in which the principal actor is hypnotized, because in such a state he can be less inhibited and more open to suggestion, with greater access to his unconscious. As in psychodrama the individual may express himself with inordinate but acceptable freedom in respect to the people with whom he is interacting. In possession these are the actual members of his community with whom he interacts every day, in contrast to psychodrama, in which the participants are just actors. The opportunity to express oneself so freely on special occasions, during which one is the center of attention while speaking one's mind, must make conforming to normal social restrictions more palatable.

Wittkower stresses the fact that possession serves not only the needs of the id, but also has superego effects. This mechanism has been seen in the use of the deity to explain or justify the behavior of one's self and others which would be unacceptable under normal circumstances. A very explicit example of this is a case in which a woman's refusal to have her sick child admitted to the hospital may have caused his death. Almost out of her mind with self-recrimination she went into non-ceremonial possession during which her Loa said that the child's soul had already been sold, meaning that the mother was free from blame (1964: 77-78).

Most devotees wait for their gods with awe and excitement, visualizing them and sensing their growing presence as the deity pervades their consciousness. If an incorrect deity comes, he is asked to leave and return at his proper time in order not to disrupt the ceremony. However, some people may be observed to resist possession. Also some individuals seem to be experiencing pain or displeasure. In such cases one may assume that ego opposition to the invading freed impulses has remained during the state of possession, and in consequence the invasion by these impulses has given rise to mental discomfort and anxiety (Wittkower 1964: 78). It is also possible that these people may be punishing themselves for some guilt that they feel.

Folk theory in Dutch Guiana in particular can account for such conflicts. The possession mechanism is similar to that in Haiti, in which the 'gros-bon-ange' is replaced by a Loa. In Dutch Guiana, however, a strong 'akra', equivalent of the 'gros-bon-ange', can dispute the right of a Winti or deity to come to the individual. The Winti therefore harasses the individual and brings him illness (Herskovits 1966: 269). It seems then that the 'akra' is replaced by the Winti in possession. The 'akra', however, unlike the 'gros-bon-ange', may make demands of the person, which must be placated, and it must be feasted. If the 'akra' remains displeased, the individual may dialogue with it, in a light possession-like state, to ascertain what it wants. If the 'akra' will not be placated the powerful Winti of a diviner may be called to take it in hand. A very strong and excited 'akra' may beat the wintiman or diviner (Herskovits 1966: 270-274). Such events seem to indicate a clear case, in folk terms, of ego resistance to the expression of normally unconscious tendencies. The ego will not let down its defenses to allow the suppressed material to come to the fore, or it erects further barriers against it.

In Dutch Guiana laws have made dancing for one's Winti very difficult. Services are permitted in Paramaribo only four times per year. Winti are usually reasonable and will accept food and wait until the devotee can worship them properly. A Winti may suddenly possess a person who denies it expression in not dancing for it, or not giving it full release. The Winti may also make his devotee so ill-tempered that he tears his clothes and breaks up whatever is in the house. The Guyanese believe that people who continually deny their Winti an outlet in dancing will go insane (Herskovits 1966: 295-230).

The implication of the preceding seems to be that the needs, impulses, and desires represented by the Winti must be expressed in some manner for the sake of the mental health of the individual involved. There is a culturally provided institution for such self-expression, but its use has been restricted with no alternative provided. Most people can manage to prevent such behavior from coming to the fore by the tactic of bargaining with the Winti, or really by assuring themselves that at some more convenient time they will be able to express themselves freely. If they continue to deny expression to the Winti their anxiety builds to produce illness or ill-temperedness. If this continues, these impulses may force recognition by bursting out in culturally unacceptable form, hence the subject is considered insane.

The Balinese seem to realize that these individual needs must be freely expressed for the well-being of the person, as indicated in their comments about an entranced pig impersonator. He had a crying fit and tantrum because someone insulted him by spitting on him. People tried to calm him but some said it was not right for him to return to normal yet because he had not yet played enough. Normally when he had had enough he would come out of the trance as soon as caught, but the insult had upset everything (Belo 1960: 209).

The determining factors in the selection of a personal deity are family heritage, which significant adults of the extended or nuclear family have been possessed by which deities and their interpretations of them, and individual personality traits (Ravenscroft 1965: 171). Family inheritance of one's deity may not be as limiting as it seems since the family in question is the extended family, thus numerous deities may be represented. It is reasonable that during the socialization process a child will acquire character traits similar to those of the adults who surround and teach him. In Dutch Guiana the child already has a Winti but can not serve it until the current devotee can no longer do so (Herskovits 1966: 291-292).

Thus the individual may choose any deity in the family, or circumstances may give him one not already in the family. His personal deity or repertoire of deities reflects his personal response to developmental factors and to exposure to the religious system of the community. The deity to whom a person is dedicated must be the correct one to allow him to express himself as fully as possible. If not there will be problems and the correct deity will have to be identified and installed. That is, the deity will not have been correct to allow the individual to express the tendencies which were pressing for expression, and this must be permitted in the choice of the new deity. Such mistakes are usually avoided by the joint efforts of the devotee and the diviner. Members of the society realize that one's deity suits his character, usually in a complementary way, as Maupoil ascertained. "... jusqu'à quel point le vodû vient-il en vous? Jusqu'à quel point votre propre désir ne le crée-t-il pas? Un vieillard me répondit: ... l'objet du désir, tel est le vodû de chacun." (... to what extent does the vodun come into you? To what extent does your own desire create it? An old man responded: ... the object of your own desire, such is the vodun of each person — author's translation.) (Bastide 1953: 53).

Two deities may vie for the same individual (Maximilien 1945: 84). This must indicate that conflicting sets of tendencies are struggling for expression. The winning deity determines which characteristics come to the fore. He will be the unique possessing deity or the principal deity in a hierarchical repertoire. When a person has only one deity, as in Bahia, at times others may spontaneously possess him in a ceremony, but this disruptive deity is usually sent away. It represents the attempt of another aspect of the personality to gain expression.

In Haiti a person whose possessions begin and end with difficulty and violence or who becomes possessed at inopportune moments, such as in the midst of some activity which requires conscious attention, is not considered worthy of his Loa, or does not know how to control him. In the former case he is being warned to improve his behavior, and in the latter he needs to undergo a ceremony to strengthen his ties with his deity. Such characteristics are also common to the Candomblé.

All possession behavior is not continuous with the devotee's conscious motivation. The deities sometimes punish their devotees, causing them to inflict pain upon themselves, or cause them to do things which, upon returning to normal, they consider contrary to their will. People may be possessed when they consciously intend to avoid such an occurrence, and the deity comes with even greater violence than when his presence is desired. The reasons given for not wanting to get possessed are often superficial, and most apparently discontinuous behavior is probably related to a fundamental, but not necessarily conscious, continuity of motivation. Thus, over time, even through different deity personalities and negative experiences, the individual manifests a basic continuity of motivation (Bourguignon 1965: 53-54). Most individuals are possessed year after year by the same deity or deities, with whose behavior patterns they are identified from the time of the initial possession.

In Haiti, Bahia, and the Zar cult, people are known for their deities, and they identify themselves with reference to them, such as Vera de Obatalá, Maria de Shango, etc. They are known for their particular portrayals of the deities as they are known for their ability as fishermen, raconteurs, etc. They may brag about their deities, being proud to be possessed by such important and powerful forces. This is, of course, quite reasonable in view of the lowly stations in life of the majority of the devotees, and the fact that most of them are women, and thus always subordinate. Not only can they express themselves freely, but they can also gain popularity among cult members and spectators.

Some people, however, may be ashamed of their possessed role. Upwardly mobile people in Trinidad, and probably the other areas also, resist possession because they consider it undignified and below them, but also because they are afraid of embarrassing themselves (Mischel and Mischel 1958: 258). An example from Recife (Brazil) indicates that they may have the right idea. A dignified official who was very proud of the social standing he had attained habitually became possessed by Yemanjá in the Shango cult to which he belonged. In this coquettish guise he demanded love and gifts, never stopping until he was given some coins. He was always very embarrassed after his performance, as his efforts to raise himself on the social ladder crumbled in a minute because his goddess begged for money. His possessed behavior was thus detrimental to a man in his position. He eventually asked to be transferred to a small rural town (Bastide 1950: 252).

The initiate knows the history and behavior of his deity and why he is worshipped. He has seen people possessed by the deity and knows how they were treated (Rodrigues 1935: 115). Because they are identified with their deities the devotees are thought, especially in Bahia, to repeat the gestures of the gods in their daily life in addition to in the ceremonial possession drama. There is a perpetual action and reaction of the individual and the cultural. The deity's personality is fixed in the more or less conscious mind of the devotee and the devotee is destined to be like the deity because the latter is his principal object of desire. As the devotee goes through the motions of being and relating to the deity in the periodic ritual of acting out the deity's myths in dance, the character of the deity imposes itself more and more on him. Thus there is an indigenous belief in the interaction between the personality of the individual and that of his deity, since the deity's personality is expressed with individuality by each devotee as a compromise between the two personalities. A person's deity is supposed to fit his personality and certain character traits are expected from people who have certain deities. The individual is like the crossroads between two worlds, that of his own personality and that of his deity's (Bastide 1958: 223-224).

It is thus believed that the devotees in their everyday lives form a sort of brotherhood, and in some places the devotees of a same deity may not intermarry. They are thought to really share the deity's character. As the Haitians say: "temperament mun, ce temperament loa-li" (the character of a person is the character of his Loa) (Wittkower 1964: 76). This should not be seen as a contradiction of what has been said about the god personality's reflecting a hidden element of that of the individual. Each individual acts out his deity in his own idiosyncratic way, thus expressing his own personal desires, yet the deity does have a basic personality recognizable across the individual variations. None of the authors mentions how great this individual variation is, but the fact that Maya Deren's (1953) possession by Erzulie, of whom she had only a general knowledge, was considered correct, would seem to indicate that there is much personal leeway.

Some authors report that certain deities tend to be manifest in specific types of people. Mischel reports that Ogun, god of war and an important deity in Trinidad, who always appears first, and is powerful and aggressive, is usually manifest in a large, stout woman. Osain, quiet, herbalist, and god of the jungle, is usually manifest in both men and slim young women (1953: 53). The latter statement is vague, the former seems reasonable, but neither seems particularly meaningful. The fact that a woman is stout need not mean that she is or wants to be aggressive. Deren reports that the deities choose devotees in whom they may be manifest to best advantage. For example, Erzulie, the beautiful goddess of love, will choose a beautiful young woman in whom she may appear at her best (1953: 230). It seems, however, that since the deity's choosing of his devotee is in reality the individual's finding of a deity to fulfill his desires, someone who is not young and beautiful would be more likely to become the beautiful goddess of love for a few moments. The stout lady Mischel would expect to see as Ogun might rather be Erzulie.

It is more important to consider profound psychological characteristics than superficial physical characteristics. People who can not normally express enough of their aggressivity may become the aggressive Ogun, and the masochists, Omolu, god of smallpox and covered with blisters. Yemanjá and Oshun offer two forms of genital love, more and less moral. In playing one of these roles one may satisfy strong desires for which life does not always offer an outlet (Bastide 1950: 252). Most of the men of the Candomblé are recognized homosexuals, since serving the Orisha is a female function. They are usually devotees of Yansan, the warrior sister or wife of Shango. She is an aggressive, restless woman with much sex life, who tries to attract many men (Carneiro 1943: 140; Landes 1940: 395). Men may be possessed by female deities and females by male deities (the latter being quite common since most of the devotees are women and most of deities males) without necessarily indicating homosexuality. The men may wish to be dependent and the women would probably like to be in a position to be more aggressive and achieve more on their own.

Thus there are similarities as well as differences among people who are devotees of the same deity, but people who are possessed by the same deity are usually seen in folk theory as having similar character traits. In Bahia, devotees of Ogun are thought of as good workers, those of Shango as turbulent and adventuresome, those of Oshun as vain and unfaithful, those of Ode as austere, those of Orishalá as extremely good and tolerant, etc. The facts may not completely justify this idea. However, the character of the god is a model of behavior for the devotees, and they train themselves to some degree to conform with these mythical and mystical norms. Some people acquire their deities at birth because their mothers have promised the deity who relieved their barrenness that the child would belong to him. Proof is sought by divination that the deity really wants the individual as his devotee. Such individuals are then shaped by their own expectations and those of their family and friends. People also probably tend to look for the similarities more than the differences, like people born under the same sign of the Zodiac. Other people and the devotees themselves expect certain things from the devotees of a particular god. Hence the idea of the god helps form the character of the person (Bastide 1958: 29, 32; 1960: 524-525).

Ravenscroft, particularly referring to Haiti, stresses the fact that there is a radical difference between a person's normal personality and his possession state god personality. The actions, speech, memory content, carriage, facial expressions, etc., are strikingly different. The disparity is so great beyond the culturally stylized movements, dress, and appetites, that it seems reasonable to hypothesize that the personality of the god represents a totally new integrative principle. In possession a totally new personality with full depth, breadth, and resilience emerges. There can be as many of these personalities as there are gods who possess the individual (1965: 167-168). This attitude is quite consistent with what was previously said in the chapter on hypnosis. The personality of the god is analogous to the ego subsystem produced in hypnosis.

Still in reference to the Haitians, but the same principle is applicable to the other groups, Ravenscroft states that the god personalities are more similar to each other than to any Haitian peasant personality type. The average Haitian peasant, no matter how different he is from his fellows in certain respects, has the same basic personality traits with regard to dominance and submission, dependence and independence, activity and passivity, along the lines determined by socialization into the traditional patterns. The gods also share the same basic personality traits among themselves. They are self-assertive, independent, dominant, occasionally aggressive, and licentious. They are authoritative, demand respect and obedience, and enjoy lording it over others, playing among themselves, and vying for dominance among their peers. They are privileged to gratify social, sexual, and aggressive needs, and are omnipotent and feared. They epitomize the Haitian peasant's conception of the perfect personality, behaving as most peasants would like to be able to behave. The gods behave in ways inaccessible to these peasants because such behavior under normal circumstances would present a threat to social control or cause personal anxiety among these people at the very bottom of a stratified society (Ravenscroft 1965: 168-169).

Recent developments have been such in these possession cults that possession is not always by a culturally prescribed deity. According to Ravenscroft, this suggests that a world view legitimizing possession and a psychological predisposition to it can result in rare or idiosyncratic forms of possession as well as the more traditional institutionalized forms. The nature of partially sanctioned, partially deviant forms reflects both the individual's strong predisposition to possession and the fact that he has particularly strong personal needs that are seeking expression (1965: 180).

In Haiti it is possible to be possessed by someone recently dead or estranged. This is recognized in the belief system but very rare, and the possessing agent is usually a loved one. The subject's behavior becomes like that of the dead person. He can not speak until that individual's soul is called from where it is residing, and then his speech is that of the dead person. In the same vein, a girl may be possessed by the soul of a lover who has jilted her (Ravenscroft 1965: 180-181).

The fact of being possessed by newly invented deities seems to indicate that new conditions are arising in the society for which the old forms are not sufficient. In Haiti, for example, new deities and families of deities have come into existence to reflect uniquely Haitian experience in contrast to the West African experiences of which the original Haitian Vodun deities were a product. Many of the women studied by Douyon, as will be discussed at more length in a subsequent chapter, have their own private possessing entities not at all related to the traditional ones. In Brazil the new cults and non-traditional versions of older ones invent new deities.

Among the Songhay a whole new class of deities came into being in the 1920's. The Haouka were supposedly brought from the Red Sea area (locus of the Zar cult) by Haussa tribesmen returning from Mecca. When the Haouka began possessing people in regular Holey ceremonies, they were felt to be hitherto unknown Holey. Their ranks consisted of characters from the impinging European civilization such as kings, governors, judges, secretaries, etc. New Haouka frequently manifested themselves. The Islamic marabouts and the Holey in the persons of their devotees strongly opposed these new deities. Possession by them was forbidden, but they continued to come, and by the truth of their prophecies, plus their persistence, they established proof of their validity. The hostility toward them lessened over a period of ten years, and the Haouka came to be considered younger siblings of Dongo, Holey of thunder. He protected them when they came in Holey ceremonies. Mainly men are possessed by the violent Haouka, whereas women are usually possessed by the traditional Holey (Rouch 1960: 73-76).

I would suggest that these new deities were able to force their way to recognition by possessing people despite the ban on them because the European colonialist influence on the Songhay created new social and psychological disequilibria to which the Haouka were a partial response. It was probably the men who felt this pressure most severely, but they did not have traditional religious outlets for it. Possession by these new genies of Western character was a way for them to incorporate the new influences into their accustomed scheme of life and deal with them on a symbolic level, if they could not totally comprehend them on a profane, everyday level. In traditional societies with the institution of spirit possession it would seem that an easy and acceptable way to introduce innovative ideas, attitudes, and techniques would be to make the possessing deities the agents of innovation. This epoch among the Songhay was undoubtedly a period of great need for innovation, and the intervention of a new set of deities was perhaps the most efficient way to effect such changes, and the way most consistent with traditional social institutions.

In thinking about the individual and possession I am led to pose some questions not considered in any of the literature. Given that a person may express various aspects of his deity or deities in different possessions, do these differences correlate with factors externally imposed, or are they rather the result of the devotees's feelings and attitudes of the moment? Are spontaneous possessions in crisis situations of the same form as ceremonial possessions? If not, how do they differ? It would also be interesting to compare the different interpretations of particular deities by different people to see what can be learned about the individual and the society from the similarities and differences in interpretation.

CHAPTER SEVEN

SOCIAL VALUE OF POSSESSION

The phenomenon of ceremonial possession is very important for the functioning of the society of which it is a part. One valuable role it plays is in providing entertainment and aesthetic interest for people whose normal lives are in many cases quite routine. Belo comments that the Balinese appear happiest when they are able to live in a steady stream of religious activities (1960: 79). In Haiti, outside of strictly ritual occasions, Vodun dances may be of half religious and half social importance. The people have a chance to laugh, enjoy themselves, and forget their troubles. The preparation itself allows them to forget their worries whether the occasion is mainly religious or mainly social. Their anxiety increases when there is no dance for a long time because of lack of money or because of police restrictions. The Haitian peasants will make great sacrifices to have a dance and rid themselves of this anxiety. They will enjoy themselves in making the gods happy and then be doubly blessed as the content deities ensure their well-being. They are happy not just because of the aesthetic pleasure engendered, but also because they are involved in creative preparation for an occasion which will bring social unity, individual and community well-being, material prosperity, and the favor of the gods.

Western mysticism is individualistic, calm, contemplative, and Apollonian. Much primitive mysticism, on the other hand, tends to be gregarious, based on collective enthusiasm, and Dionysian (Mars 1951: 645). In such primitive religious ceremonies all factors combine to produce a dramatic social atmosphere and mentality which redefines reality. Individual thoughts and feelings are transcended by collective action and sentiment, and individual attention changes to collective preoccupation. Group thought focuses on the principle of the god or gods being served and the secular world is forgotten (Ravenscroft 1965: 170).

According to Maximilien, himself a Haitian, in order to become possessed at all, and particularly to rise in the traditional religious hierarchy, the devotee must get rid of the illusion of the personal ego. It must lose its power to impose itself on his soul as a reality. He must feel himself a part of the all. All beings must live and breathe in him as he lives and breathes in them. He learns more about reality as he understands his role in the economy of nature and in community religious life. He becomes less superstitious and more knowledgeable than people who are not involved in the religion. It is the people who are not involved in the collective nature of the religious system who are more superstitious and who tend to resort more to magical methods to control reality. The collective religion both defines reality and provides its devotees with the means to deal with it (1945: 85-86).

Ceremonial possession is both built upon group solidarity, in that it is largely a result of the cultural determinism of the society's collective representations, and is a promoter of this social solidarity. The individual becomes aware of his interdependence with the members of the society and the mutuality of their destinies. Both he and they realize that what each is doing can only be for oneself and others simultaneously. Collective models, meanings, and responses alone can give meaning to the individual's manifestations, and individuals who personify the deities do so for the entire community as well as for themselves.

This ceremonial possession provides a perfect example of Victor Turner's concept of 'communitas'. The normal distinctions of the everyday society are abolished, and the laws governing the new communitas are ultimate in the culture — those of the deified ancestors, the founders of the society (1968). Social distinctions between people are erased, as are even those between oneself and others to some degree, as all, high and low, are transferred from the level of ordinary, human, structured interaction to the level of supernatural interaction. Those who do not become gods participate in their glory and power by interacting with them, and thus in a sense gaining a degree of control over them.

During this sacred liminal period with all normal structure in abeyance, the individuals lose their normal identities. The people who are structurally powerless and inferior socially (most people who get possessed are, as has been noted, women) are in their glory because they bring great benefits to the community by personifying and pleasing the gods. Because of their lowly position in the normal society it is probably quite easy for them to give up their own uninflated egos to play such exalted roles.

In this communitas period, characterized by generalization and de-differentiation of all external relations, one's internal psychological apparatus may become de-differentiated and free (Turner 1968).

There is no longer any need to repress the material repressed in accordance with normal social relations and the individual may express his whole self. This is done within the limits of the sacred values of the situation, of course, but much more freedom of personal expression is provided during this period, with fewer adverse, and more positive consequences than in the normal course of things. There is never a complete lack of structure, or anarchy would reign, which is not the case; but the structure is more subtle, and organized according to sacred rather than secular values. Each man is thus culturally permitted to express his total self, or at least a great deal of it, because he can express the opposite and complementary aspects in the communitas period of that which he expresses in normal, structured, everyday life. Ceremonial possession and also the Carnival in Brazil and the Caribbean are exemplary of the communitas period.

Both possession and Carnival can be likened to rituals of rebellion, in that behavior forbidden under normal circumstances is the norm during these periods. Such situations can be analogised on a societal level to the psychological phenomenon previously discussed in relation to hypnosis and possession. The ego temporarily lets down its defenses and relinquishes control to a subsystem which may allow expression of tendencies not normally expressed. The ability to do so is evidence of a strong ego, because the ego only relinquishes control because it is able to resume it when necessary or desirable. The ego is strengthened in the process because potentially disruptive tendencies are given expression and thus need not, in being frustrated and suppressed, threaten the whole organization of the ego. It is noted by Dr. Lamarck Douyon, Haitian psychiatrist, that the population of mental hospitals in countries such as Trinidad decreases after a successful Carnival. Thus many people get rid of their neurotic problems, at least temporarily, because they are allowed to express them openly (1968: 27). It would seem that more opportunities for institutionalized regression in the service of the ego, of which this is a good example, would be very useful in reducing the number of private neurotic manifestations in any society. Rather than to perform private idiosyncratic rituals the individual could participate usefully in collective, socially meaningful rituals, and be a more normally functioning member of the society.

In possession ceremonies and in the Carnival, the society, like the personalities of the participants, relinquishes normal control to these societal subsystems for a specific period of time. During this time people can give vent to their antisocial desires. Because they are permitted this approved catharsis, which they may anticipate until its periodic occurrence, it is easier for them to accept normal social regulations, thus the social organization is strengthened. In Brazil, for example, millions of people live in abject poverty alongside fabulous wealth. Once a year, however, social distinctions are ostensibly forgotten. The rich and powerful let down their hair and the poor may act out their fantasy lives as they dance in the streets. Many of the rich now do their celebrating in private clubs and merely watch the festivities in the streets rather than actually mingling, but nevertheless the poor are kings and queens for a while. The latter spend all year preparing for these few days during which they will wear the beautiful costumes which they have made enormous sacrifices to have, and be the center of attention as they become the personages of their fantasy world. During this time they can express their pent-up hostilities and jealousies against the establishment and those who profit from it, but they can also, for a while, participate in its luxury and splendor. Also, many of these poor people belong to one of the various spiritist religions, of diverse origins and degrees of syncretism, in which they can periodically transcend their lowly status by becoming, or at least directly communicating with, gods. Hence they have periodic releases on a smaller scale during the year in addition to this society-wide release once a year.

Possession ceremonies can also contribute to social solidarity and stability by providing collective, public opportunities, with supernatural sanction, to punish people for antisocial behavior in their daily lives. Such punishment can be effected in the Candomblé by the use of magic or of songs of punishment played and sung during public ceremonies. They produce brutal, tiring, and painful possessions, thus inducing the individual to correct his subsequent behavior (Bastide 1960: 317). The violence of such possessions is probably the result of the combined effect of both the condemning social suggestion and the guilt and shame felt by the individual for having performed such acts of which everyone is aware. The brutality of the possession in itself is seen as punishment by the devotee's god for his behavior. Combining psychological, social, and supernatural condemnation, this is probably a very good inducement to correct conduct.

Also, in possession ceremonies direct statements may be made to disruptive persons by possessed individuals. Such statements carry great weight because they are pronounced by the gods. In a Balinese village example reported by Belo, an entranced man voiced the prevalent antagonism felt by most members of the community toward one of their number. He was apparently not so unconscious as to be unaware of the preoccupation he shared with the rest of the group. As a spokesman of the gods he was supposed to be in some way responsible for the welfare of the community. It was up to him to make pronouncements of the god's will to restore peace and harmony (1960: 147).

Possession ceremonies may also be contributory to social stability by concentrating on points of strain in the structure of the society. This is evidenced in the N'Deup cult found in Senegal. N'Deup ceremonies are organized for various reasons. Fear and anger in individuals and groups disrupt social equilibrium. Thus, whether the disequilibrium concerns an individual or is symptomatic of a social crisis, an N'Deup manifestation is deemed necessary. The N'Deup ceremony is designed to re-establish an order of which man is the master. The victim of any crisis or disturbance must be integrated or re-integrated into the community, and it must retain its stability (Samb 1967: 28-29).

Polygamy is a social institution which frequently provokes problems and makes an N'Deup ceremony necessary. A man takes a second wife. The first waits a while and then, excessively jealous, has a hysterical attack. An n'deup-kat (priest) is called to set a time for the ceremony (Samb 1967: 29). As in all ceremonies of this type there must be elaborate and expensive preparations for which the disturbed woman is the cause and excuse, and thus the center of attention — the queen for a few days, as it were.

The ceremony lasts for three or more days, during which people dance and get possessed. An animal is sacrificed and some blood put on the 'sick' woman, this blood creating a link between herself and a genie, making him her guardian spirit. Distinguished by special markings she is possessed by the genie for a day and a night. She is temporarily outside the pale of ordinary life, as shown by her new status as a woman linked to the gods (Samb 1967: 32).

The function of the possession dance is to obtain the necessary agreement and co-operation to restore the health of the individual and the strength and integration of the community, and to rid man of his feeling of helpless weakness in the face of disruption (Samb 1967: 33). This is the tactic used by healers in many traditional societies. When a person is disturbed or ill his or her problem is considered to be not just an individual, localized problem. It is rather a problem concerning the total person, psyche and soma, as well as the other members of the community with whom the individual interacts. Since the individual is seen not merely as a cipher but as an organically integrated and important member of the community, his or her well-being or lack of it is of concern to the whole community. As in the N'Deup, the person's apparent organically or psychologically caused illness may conceivably be the result of strained social interaction, and it is in large part treated as such.

The afflicted individual is made the center of attention, which is very important since he, or usually she, has probably been suffering from a lack of attention. He is given the feeling of importance that he needs. He may be asked to voice his complaints about other members of the community, and they about him. One common source of such trouble, as in the N'Deup and also in the Zar cult, is the institution of polygamy, which is why most members are women. The woman's illness is usually resolved by her being made a member of a cult in which she receives the sense of self-worth and social prestige which has been lacking. Thus illnesses are seen to be the product of somatic, psychological, and social forces, and are treated on these levels, resulting in benefits for both the individual and the society. Such tactics enhance social solidarity and stability by eliminating potentially disruptive forces in a constructive manner. This is an efficacious prototype of Jacob Moreno's psychodrama and sociodrama techniques. The traditional method has the advantage, which Moreno's methods lack, of being set in its natural habitat with the actual actors involved.

Possession ceremonies then, can be seen as both individual and group therapy, prophylactic and/or curative, with the priest as therapist. I am not implying that the people who participate are in any way mentally disturbed, because I do not believe that this is usually the case. The individuals who participate and freely express themselves in the supreme sacred act of their society undoubtedly come out of it with a great sense of well-being, personally beneficial for them and conducive to good interaction with others. The well-being of the total community is thus assured.

The essential religious meaning of such possession rituals is in the establishment of a means of communication with the gods (Bowers 1961: 272). They are temporarily members of the community so that man can deal with them (Linton 1956: 128). Man and his deities are now, in a sense, on the same plane. Thus the communitas period even obliterates the line between natural and supernatural, sacred and profane, as men and gods are fused in the possession phenomenon. Man is elevated to a divine plane because he incarnates the gods, and interacts with them, but they also come down to a human plane by virtue of being embodied in men. The gods-incarnate are treated with both respect as gods to be supplicated, and banter as equals or deities who have come to enjoy themselves in a very human manner. In communicating with the gods in this manner the humans can feel a sense of security because they are in direct contact with the powers that control their lives. They are taking active and positive steps to insure the well-being of individuals and the community by this collective evoking of the gods, and they are taking positive, constructive action in creating an order of which men are in control, rather than helpless.

CHAPTER EIGHT

POSSESSION, MENTAL ILLNESS, AND THERAPY

There is much discussion and disagreement about whether possession is indicative of the normality or abnormality of the individuals involved. This topic is discussed in a subsequent chapter. In this chapter I am concerned with showing the relationship between possession, mental illness, and therapy in native and Western terms. Most of the groups studied distinguish perfectly clearly between plain, undirected insanity, and spirit possession. Insanity is regarded as a disease and treated as such. Field reports that the Gã of Ghana often ask if an individual has had a vision or supernatural experience, or if he is simply insane (1961: 102).

Most of the recent works about spirit possession insist on the fact that in their private lives the people who become possessed show no signs of being unbalanced or neurotic. They usually appear to be in good physical and mental health, and are usually, especially the priests and priestesses, quite intelligent people (Metraux 1958; Field 1961; Stainbrook 1952; Herskovits 1937). When excited by the spirit they are undoubtedly working off a great deal of steam of which others must dispose quietly, and probably less satisfactorily. Field points out that the Gã system of spirit possession is probably quite efficient from the point of view of Western medicine, in addition to having the social value of providing dignified niches for types of people who in Western society would be misfits and plagues of the society (1961: 108-109).

It is necessary to insist upon the normality of the phenomenon of possession because the behavioral manifestations fall within the traditional Western definitions of pathological behavior. However, the truth is that the mechanisms involved may be reflective of normality as well as of pathology depending upon various factors, as shall be seen. Since the cultures to which these possession cults belong clearly distinguish between normal and abnormal processes, the investigator should respect this distinction and try to understand it in its own terms rather than to impose his categories and conclude with an incorrect understanding of the society he purports to know. This would seem to be a much more reasonable approach than to consider the whole phenomenon as abnormal merely because it is considered so in Western society. There is no reason to feel that the viewpoint of Western society is the only valid one, supposedly a basic premise of anthropological relativity, and in many instances it may be much less valid than others in facilitating the satisfactory integration of individual and society.

Of the groups with which I am principally concerned, only in the Zar cult (like the N'Deup) is illness the main reason given for joining. In all of the other societies possession is the supreme act of worship of the gods and divinized ancestors of the group. People do not usually become members as a cure for their illnesses, but by initiation into the ways and needs of the deity who has chosen the devotee as his own. De Heusch states that in Dahomey, for example, illness or trouble in the family may indicate that a Vodun wants to be served by that family, but the person chosen to serve the Vodun is often not the one who had the illness or trouble, thus this devotee can not have joined for personal therapy (1965: 152). According to Leiris, however, even in the Zar cult there are both normal people and people with some degree of psychological disturbance who get possessed (1958: 28). Hence it seems evident that possession is not either merely culturally accepted role playing or pathology, but may be one or the other for different individuals and under different circumstances.

I think that this distinction between the Zar cult and the others represents explanations given by different cultures of the same phenomenon rather than two distinct phenomena. What is described as illness in the Zar cult is the same as the signs that the gods want to be served in the other societies. The person in question becomes very withdrawn or hysterical, or each alternately. This is the same mechanism whether considered illness, a call from the gods, or the result of having an unsocialized or angry and neglected god.

From what I gather from the literature on the Zar cult, the reason for the differences in perspective lies in the different nature of the social institutions involved in Ethiopia as opposed to the other areas. In the other societies being considered, the possessing entities are the gods of the community who have come to enjoy themselves and help the members of the group. Thus possession of members of the society is beneficial for all, and these people are fulfilling a most essential community service. By working out any antisocial tendencies they may have in a socially acceptable and useful way, they are serving the cause of social solidarity.

The Zar cult, on the contrary, is not an integral part of a total community. It is not the religious institution of a total society, but more like a separate community with its own structure, composed of people for whom the normal community social structure does not provide satisfaction. As in all of the cults, the majority of members are women, and here the majority of priests are men. There is no institution, like the religious systems of the other societies, which allows these women, who have little range for free self-expression or the gaining of personal recognition, an opportunity to fulfill these needs. Hence they are considered sick. This 'sickness' is frequently the predominantly psychosomatic reaction to the individual's social problems or to the pressures of everyday life. The remedy for such a case is membership in a group in which everyone has been cured of the same type of malady. This cult has no direct beneficent functions for the total community as do the others in pleasing and assuring the good will of the deities of the community. However, it does indirectly work toward the well-being of the community from which these people come because after satisfying their needs by their participation in the Zar cult the devotees can function better as members of their own communities.

To return to possession, mental illness, and therapy, possession is not considered an abnormal phenomenon by the groups under consideration, but it is rather a sign of election by the gods. However, according to native theories of personality, mental illness is explained by the same mechanisms as possession. Possession may be seen as socially and psychologically controlled regression in the service of the ego. Cultural molds, plus the social value such behavior serves, provide a secure and supportive atmosphere in which such regression can beneficially take place.

Mental illness and pathological behavior may be seen as regression proper which takes uncontrollable and culturally unacceptable and idiosyncratic forms. Where the culture provides socially valued ego subsystems, such as the god personalities, which can take over the control of the devotee's faculties, we find normal regression in the service of the ego. When an individual, for some reason, can not take advantage of these forms, his regressive manifestation is regression proper and he is considered insane in the terms of his society. This idea may be applied to modern as well as primitive societies.

That the same phenomenon is involved in both spirit possession and insanity is consistent with native personality theory. In Haiti the individual has two souls, the 'gros-bon-ange' which gives the power to feel, will, and understand, and the 'petit-bon-ange', which is the guardian angel. The 'petit-bon-ange' fights off evil spirits and provides the person with warnings of danger. The 'gros-bon-ange' can leave the body, and does so in dreams, possession, and insanity. While the individual sleeps it is wandering around, and its adventures furnish the content of his dreams. In possession it is replaced by a Loa. Also a sorcerer can take it from a person's head by magic and cause insanity. He puts an animal's, thief's, epileptic's, or reincarnated dead person's spirit into the victim's head to replace the 'gros-bon-ange'. The kind of spirit involved is evident in his behavior. It replaces the 'gros-bon-ange' and overcomes the 'petit-bon-ange', thus taking control of the victim's total being. This is one of the main causes of supernatural 'folie' or insanity. Another cause is that an angry Loa may supplant the 'gros-bon-ange' and refuse to leave the victim's head until he, frequently someone who has become a Christian, accepts Vodun and agrees to worship the Loa. His acceptance does not guarantee the end of his illness (Kiev 1961a: 261; 1961 b: 135-136).

Analogously, among the Songhay the Holey can push one soul out of place and replace it so that the man's body is commanded by the deity. People who are considered insane in a fashion usually incurable are possessed by the 'angels of satan' or demons. The Songhay indicate the normality of possession by the Holey by only using the term sick for the pre-initiation possession when the Holey has not been socialized, and at which point the person may actually remain sick if he is not initiated. After initiation the devotee is considered normal. The brutality of these seizures is not condemned because it is the Holey whose behavior is manifest, and man has no right to judge the deities (Rouch 1960: 21, 26, 189). In the Zar cult also, people considered insane are felt to be possessed by demons or unsocialized Zar. There are also people who have pathological seizures resembling Zar possession, but such people are not cult members (Leiris 1958: 29-20). Thus there is a clear distinction between insanity resembling possession or pre-initiation phenomena, and normal possession. The determining factor is whether this manifestation becomes socialized. If it does, the individual becomes the devotee of a god, if not he is insane.

In the Haitian belief system there are two kinds of illness, natural and supernatural. Natural folie consists of calm behavior and a refusal to talk and eat. It may last up to eight months. It may be treated by a houngan, mambo (priestess), leaf doctor, or physician. This category includes everything from infectious diseases to chronic degenerative diseases. It may only be cured in the early stages, and is due to severe frustrations in life, weakness of the brain, too much intellectual effort, or certain unfulfilled ambitions. It is also characterized by the departure of the 'gros-bon-ange'. Hereditary folie due to congenital defects or mental deficiency is incurable, as the wise and honorable houngan will admit (Kiev 1961b: 261).

Supernatural folie is manifest in excitement, excessive talking and aggressiveness, and tearing one's clothes. It is usually short-lived, sometimes only several days. It is attributed to the magic of a sorcerer, or to an angry Loa. It may only be treated by a houngan or mambo, who must first determine by divination if it is of natural or supernatural origin. To do this he or she relies heavily on paid informants, the patient's kin, and the patient himself for a detailed account of his activities to see if he has offended an individual or a Loa who may now be seeking revenge. To be cured the person must have faith in God, Vodun, and the houngan, thus if he is not cured this may be attributed to his lack of faith in any of the three (Kiev 1961b: 261).

Folie differs from regular ceremonial possession in that the individual can not be brought out of his state by ordinary ritual means (Kiev 1961b: 261). In both cases, however, the person's behavior is so different from the usual that it appears to be caused by a different personality, as Americans implicitly recognize when they ask people 'what has gotten into them' or 'what has possessed them' to account for certain unexpected behavior. The close relationship between folie and ceremonial possession is evident in the commonly stated fact that the first indications that a person is being called to become a devotee, and particularly that a man is being called to be a priest, are indistinguishable from folie. If the person does not respond to the call he may be punished in the form of insanity or illness. This seems to be the case in most possession and shamanic phenomena. If a person prone to such seizures can not control them by fitting them into some culturally prescribed pattern, for any reason, he is then ill according to the definitions of his culture.

Field cites the case of a Christian Gã woman who used to have hysterics in church. She was diagnosed as taken by the spirits and advised to train as a woyo, the devotee of a Gã deity. Because of her

Christian beliefs she refused, at which point she became more or less insane, deaf, and dumb. When she yielded and began training as a woyo her symptoms left. The Christian church persuaded her to come back and her malady reappeared. She wavered back and forth but finally yielded and became a woyo (1961: 101). This type of case can probably be reported for any of the groups in question and probably many other situations in which a person is torn between expressing himself in the manner of the traditional religion and joining an established church.

Thus the individual must either accept the call of the deities or be insane. In Haiti, the person considered most prone to such folie is the houngan because of his enormous responsibility to the Loa. If he forgets to honor them or forgets something in a ceremony he may lose his power and become insane. Another houngan may cause folie by sending an evil spirit to overcome him. If an assistant can not cure him by various ceremonial means, he dies. Some men who want to become houngans buy the post by paying another to teach them. They may not be able to control the power they have bought and subsequently become insane (Kiev 1961a: 263).

Vodun theories of psychopathology and its treatment derive logically from native notions of personality configuration (Kiev 1961a: 264). If we take psychiatry to mean a system of treatment for disorders of thought, mood, and behavior, based on the theoretical conception of normal behavior, then the model presented by Vodun fits the description well. Vodun theory offers acceptable notions of etiology, disease descriptions, dynamic and economical analyses, plus ideas about heredity, patient responsibility, prognosis, and treatment. Wise houngans can make a number of diagnoses comparable to Western classification. They are familiar with symptoms suggestive of depression, dementia praecox, acute schizophrenia, acute mania, hysteria, paranoia, and mental deficiency. They recognize, within their own theoretical and technological limits, which illnesses can and can not be cured. Kiev thus feels that the houngan's functions meet the criteria for psychotherapy (1961a: 264).

Rouch states that the seance of initiation among the Songhay, which must be conducted by a zima (priest), corresponds to psychoanalytic treatment, except that the zima hardly ever fails. The zima needs much knowledge of mythology, ritual, and human nature to fulfill his required functions. He must know if an illness is actually possession by the Holey, and he must know the proper method of initiating people into the service of the deities. Any failure is attributed to his ineptness (1960: 193-194, 300).

The people who desire initiation into the Zar cult are those who have had illnesses, accidents, or troubles attributable to the ill will of the Zar. In most cases the possession manifestation does not represent the original trouble, and does not take place until after the intervention of the priest or healer, who leads the Zar who is supposedly responsible for the individual's troubles to possess the victim in order to dialogue with him and try to reach an agreement. The nature of the illness, personality of the person, identity of the Zar who have possessed other members of the family, and the circumstances under which the trouble occurred are indices which allow the healer to determine which Zar is responsible. Once this provisional diagnosis is made, he brings on possession by that Zar in perfect conformity with native personality theory (Leiris 1958: 17-18). The person resolves his discord with the Zar by learning to serve him in regular, ceremonial possession. This 'illness' or trouble, the symptoms of which are usually undoubtedly largely psychosomatic, is the product of stress and personal frustration, and may be relieved by the free expression of the possession state. This type of resolution of one's problems is probably quite satisfying in that the sick person is the center of attention for a while and acquires a new status providing more self-esteem and pleasure.

In Haiti the houngan, like the zima, or the Zar healer, is relied upon for relief. He has had training in the treatment of illness, initiation procedures, and particularly in the observation of human nature. He has status and prestige in accordance with his previous success, and access to the symbolic paraphernalia of his office furthers his influence. The supernatural causes of illness and the necessity of faith for successful healing are basic explanatory tenets held by the whole community. The patient's favorable expectations are reinforced by the fact that the treatment takes place in a ceremony staged especially for him. The houngan has faith in his time-honored methods and faith in the patient's ability to respond to the treatment. He follows a definite procedure, which, according to Kiev, embodies all the dynamic features of good psychotherapeutic technique. The houngan's frequent show of initial pessimism introduces an element of ambiguity, raising the degree of anxiety and suggestibility of the patient, and increasing his desire to please the houngan. The houngan's omnipotence, and the pressure of the group on the patient to conform, are important causes of the latter's passivity. Also many patients pray and fast before healing ceremonies to increase the likelihood of success. Of course praying can increase suggestibility and fasting increases susceptibility to the neurophysiological changes inducing possession. The connection of the treatment process with the dominant values of the culture increases its therapeutic potential and enlists the valuable support of the community, which reinforces the patient's faith in the houngan (Kiev 1961a: 264).

The patient comes to the healer in a marked state of distress. His illness is confidence-destroying, humiliating, and anxiety-producing. When the illness is due to wrongdoing or the violation of a taboo, and thus sent as punishment by the gods, the sick person feels that others see him as a social menace worthy of shaming and ostracism. He loses his self-esteem and confidence in his usual manner of doing things, then turns to an acknowledged leader for help. To be cured of the wrath of the deity he must serve him by being inducted into the possession cult, or become more active in the service of the deity than previously, perhaps being elevated to a higher rank in the hierarchy of devotees.

In the treatment process the individual's sense of self-identity and self-awareness are reduced and the sense of merging with the group intensified by the emotionally charged atmosphere of group singing and clapping in unison to accompany the ministrations of the houngan. The sufferer relies on the group as well as on the houngan for relief. Emotional, attitudinal, and interpersonal aspects of the illness are emphasized (Kiev 1968: 146-147). Thus individual illness is seen as the product of social interaction. There is concentrated group pressure on the patient to get well. Since faulty conduct is usually the cause of his illness, in the treatment the community is giving him the occasion to improve and be welcomed back. It is also giving him the attention and consideration the lack of which perhaps precipitated his troubles. Thus the individual works out his problems in relation to a real social situation with people with whom he comes into daily contact.

The point of culmination is the patient's possession by the deity who has been bothering him, whom he will now learn to serve and control (Kiev 1968: 145). After this group supported cathartic experience, in which he has been the center of attention and had the satisfaction of releasing tension, he will learn to control the expression of whatever has been bothering him, and manifest it in the possession by his god in a socially approved and valuable manner. The healing situation functions like hypnotherapy in that the patient can freely express repressed material. The opportunity to express himself as the center of attention under such special conditions may also help the individual to reorder his relationships with the other members of the community, and they with him. He also now occupies a privileged social position as a devotee of the gods.

In addition to these supernatural disturbances, which can be controlled and cured by induction into a possession cult, the same mechanism as in possession is recognized as operative in the psychotic illnesses of people alienated from the traditional milieu. These people can not channel their impulses into acknowledged and useful roles as is possible in the traditional religion because their new culture provides no such roles. For example, people who have dissociated themselves from Vodun are sometimes possessed. A houngan can find out which Loa wants to be appeased in this conflict apparently centering around the person's suppressed desire to return to the freedom of expression and security of the traditional religion. If such individuals do not respond to the summons of the Loa they sometimes become insane as punishment from the Loa (Kiev 1961b: 135).

According to Haitian psychiatrists, such patients initially diagnosed as hysterical often deteriorate into chronic schizophrenia after repeated episodes. The psychotic syndrome known in Haiti as 'bouffée délirante aigue' is often accompanied by paranoid delusions based in general on Vodun themes associated with delusions of persecution. Such individuals are apparently still affected by elements of Vodun culture which call forth marked anxiety reactions. They are, however, sufficiently alienated from peasant culture as to be unable to use the means of anxiety reduction provided in the role playing of Vodun ceremonial possession (Kiev 1961b: 135). The anxiety they feel seems to be a result of ambivalent feelings about leaving and denying the peasant milieu. Although they have taken on the veneer of sophisticated Christianity they obviously still believe in the Loa. Since they will not serve them they must suffer their wrath. This correlates well with Lamarck Douyon's statement that noticeable improvements are observed in mental patients who have taken an active part in Carnival festivities. It is understandable, he continues, that 'sambatherapy' is being applied in certain experimental centers in Europe (1966: 27). The dances, masks, disguises, and Carnival activities permit people to express their normally suppressed desires and fantasies, thus paving the way to better mental health.

In Bahia, people do not distinguish between acceptable and unacceptable behavior according to the criteria of Western psychopathology. Among the lower class especially, but not uniquely, hallucinatory experiences are accepted as normally conceivable although not common. Delusional speech, particularly of a religious nature, is not part of the community definition of disordered behavior. Uncontrolled aggressive behavior, however, may lead to a person's being considered insane (Stainbrook 1952: 334).

The complex patterns of behavior institutionalized in the Candomblé may be used by different individuals in different ways for the recurring periodic gratification of several needs. Whatever needs the individual satisfies in his ceremonial behavior, he must be in sufficient control of his regressive and autistic behavior and reality testing apparatuses to perform correctly within the relatively rigid ritualistic group action. Individuals who use the dissociative behavior of possession in an idiosyncratic manner are excluded from traditional Candomblés. Successful initiation into the Candomblé is accompanied by considerable psychological screening. Traditional Yoruba Candomblés thus do not function in such a way as to allow the institutionalization of psychopathological behavior. Non-traditional Candomblés de Caboclo and the Macumba are composed of many more behaviorally deviant people and may be different in psychodynamic organization (Stainbrook 1952: 334).

In a mental hospital in Bahia, the anxieties, fears, and threats of retribution felt by the patients, especially lower class patients, are interpreted as arising from African or Catholic cultural deities, depending upon the religious background of the individual. For most of the lower class people, plus middle class women (middle class men have more secular, economic interests) delusional, megalomaniacal, and persecutory symptoms are fantasied in terms of the religious institutions of the community. The content of Candomblé behavior plays a significant role in the thoughts and actions of many female, lower class schizophrenics. Some acute schizophrenic reactions are particularly characterized by the acting out of possession by African gods or goddesses as in the Candomblé. The clinical picture of such people is definitely schizophrenic, not just hysterical, and usually occurs as a reaction to situationally acute stresses or deprivation.[1] The major psychological goal achieved in the psychotic resolution of their problems seems to be identification with the omnipotent deity, which is exactly what the traditional priestly healers do with their patients. This is similar, although in an abnormal rather than normal manner, to the temporary introjection of and identification with the god personality achieved by Candomblé participants during possession ceremonies (Stainbrook 1952: 333-334).

In absolute numbers only a small proportion, three to five per cent, of the psychiatric patients have actually been members of the Candomblé. Stainbrook does not give the total population of the hospital (1952: 333-335). This is in a population of 400,000 (1950 census) of which about 30,000 people are linked to one hundred Candomblés (Carneiro 1961: 56). An interesting correlative observation is the low incidence of gross hysterical dissociative reactions among the lower class black people of Bahia (Stainbrook 1952: 335).

This low incidence of hysteria among the people in question is probably due to the fact that they have an alternative way of expressing the tendencies that nineteenth century Europeans in particular expressed in the culturally stylized pattern of hysteria. The Africans, Afro-Americans, and others who have cults of possession seem to have a much more practical cultural institution in possession than other social groups do in hysteria. A socially valuable and psychologically satisfying outlet for normally suppressed and repressed tendencies is periodically provided in possession, in contrast with the idiosyncratic, socially unacceptable and thus psychologically unsatisfactory and sometimes harmful institution of hysteria. Hysteria and possession seem to involve similar mechanisms, the difference being that the latter is a culturally patterned phenomenon within the confines of which the individual can express normally unexpressed behavioral inclinations, whereas in the former there are no such positively evaluated patterns to guide and support the individual.

---

[1] Stainbrook notes that in 106 of the 200 randomly chosen cases of schizophrenia he studied in patients under forty years of age one or both of the patient's parents had been dead by the time the patient entered the hospital, at an average age of twenty-four. The entire population has a high mortality rate but other factors must also account for such a high proportion of bereaved individuals in the hospital population. Perhaps there is a positive correlation between schizophrenia and disturbed homes (1952: 333).

It is apparent, however, that where the cultural norms are lacking, as with the Haitians who have left the peasant milieu, such manifestations may tend more toward the form of hysteria. They may be fitted into the traditional patterns with the help of the houngan, but if this is not done the person remains ill. Thus Haitian folk theory is quite sophisticated in its understanding of human psychology. The society provides outlets for the tensions and conflicts that it engenders. The individuals who take advantage of them are normal because they work out their problems within the provided context. Others, who may have developed the same tensions and conflicts without accepting the corresponding outlets, become neurotic or even psychotic. In some cases it is the person's severely neurotic or psychotic tendencies which prohibit him from accepting the culturally provided remedies, as Haitians realize in recognizing that some types of folie are incurable. Yet others who could accept the remedies provided undoubtedly worsen their condition by not doing so because they have left the cultural milieu.

The cultural factor is so significant because it determines the way in which both the subject and the other members of the community regard his unusual state. Experiencing the unusual psychological and physiological state of possession, associated with the reduction of the regular defenses, and a change in bodily sensations, induces the individual to seek to understand an experience that can not readily be understood in ordinary, common sense terms. The cognitive dissonance engendered in the possessed person, as well as his own observation of other members of the community behaving as if they were in the control of an outside force, can not fail to impress everyone with the validity of whatever theory is at hand to explain the phenomenon. Both the possessed individual and the spectators see the houngan as omniscient, because of his ability to direct the possession manifestations. Hence, possession, in addition to allowing the individual to express himself, also lets him demonstrate the validity of the Vodun belief system (Kiev 1968: 145-148). The same holds true for the other possession cults. In the same vein, if hysteria is the explanation for such behavior, the individual and the other members of the community will act according to their theories about the nature and treatment of hysteria.

CHAPTER NINE

THE EFFECTS
OF SOCIAL DISORGANIZATION ON POSSESSION

The importance of cultural determinism in possession ceremonies has been emphasized. However, as the religious system becomes disorganized as a result of social changes, community control diminishes and individualism begins to play a greater role. In the traditional setting the content of possession manifestations is a culturally determined expression of traditional mysticism, whereas when this setting no longer prevails, possession becomes more the expression of individual complexes and fantasies.

As the myths are forgotten and group control lessens, the individual, rather than modeling himself on traditional patterns which provide support for his behavior, will be purely under the control of his own impulses and will express them in possession. These impulses will form their own expressive symbols through the individual's invention of new deities which are images of the self and its version of the reality it perceives. On this basis Bastide hypothesizes that wherever group control diminishes, mysticism changes from the expression of collective models to the individual expression of the experiences people are undergoing as a result of social changes. The trance phenomenon mirrors the degree of cohesion or disintegration of the social milieu. In psychoanalytic terms, what this means is that the traditional cults represent the triumph of the superego, that is, the collective norms, and those involving less social control represent the triumph of the ego and id, or individual self-determination (1960: 524-526).

The best documented examples of this transition from traditional social control to individual self-expression are in Brazil, as manifest in the traditional Candomblés at one pole and the Catimbó and Macumba at the other. The traditional Candomblé takes individual differences into account in furnishing an ensemble of deity personalities from which its members can choose. The number of personalities is not, of course, infinite. Both religious syncretism and destructuralization tend to multiply the number of deities. When the number of gods is increased, their individual, specific characters are lost. They are depersonalized and made into vague concepts within

which each person may express what he wants — his dreams and
desires, illusions, resentments, etc. (Bastide 1960: 526). Also, some of
the possessing figures are not deities but just other personalities, as is
often the case among the deracinated members of Vodun cults living
in Port-au-Prince studied by Douyon.

As traditional religious organization becomes weakened by social
change, and traditional control lessens, possession phenomena tend
to become not only more individualistic but also more pathological.
In Brazil only when the traditional Candomblé is being persecuted
by the government and not allowed to meet, causing the devotees to
seek religious fulfillment elsewhere in spiritist cults, do pathological
troubles appear among them. The individuals' repressed tendencies
no longer find expression as mystical manifestations in the ready-
made framework of god personalities furnished by the traditional
communities. They are rather more anarchistically expressed in less
structured cults, to the detriment of the mental health of the
participants (Bastide 1950: 251). The lessening or absence of structure
causes such disorganized possession to be more a case of regression
proper than regression in the service of the ego, as in traditional
possession.

Cultural   disorganization   then   both   causes   individual   disorganization and makes that which is potentially present more
evident. The individual becomes disorganized because he no longer
has a coherent, integrated cultural system around which to build his
world, so his personality may also be poorly integrated. Any
previously unexpressed elements of personality disorganization that
come to the fore in the absence of specific cultural patterns into
which to insert them, must be manifest idiosyncratically and perhaps
in an extreme manner. No longer channeled by social constraints
they burst forth uncontrolledly. Hence Bastide states that trance
phenomena vary from reflections of the controlled social pressure of
the group to individualistic hysterical violence, in accord with the
control of traditional organization or its breakdown (1960: 258).

An extreme case of this phenomenon can be found in Martinique.
In Martinique the African religions which are found in other parts of
the New World have been completely destroyed, thus there is no
ceremonial possession. Frequent seizures, said to be hysterical, occur
among the women, particularly from Saturday night to Sunday
morning and during Carnival. These seizures are analogous to the
normal ones which in other areas are explained by the descent of the

gods, but here the institutionalized cult has disappeared. The seizures are attributed to the actions of quimbaiseurs (sorcerers) who have the power to make demons enter into the body of their victims. The debris of the disappeared cult are metamorphosed into magical beliefs and practices (Bastide 1967: 154).

Some intermediary examples from Brazil will make more explicit the nature of this transformational process from socially controlled religious manifestations to individualism, pathology, and magic. One cult exemplifying such disorganization is the rural Catimbó in Maranhão, a basically Indian cult which many Africans joined, adding their deities and receiving important posts because of their ability to go into trances easily. There is no real organization, no priest or religious authority, just folklore. The whole village congregates once a month to call the spirits. Their mystical ecstasy is not controlled but is rather a savage deliverance from the miseries of daily existence to experience the joyful euphoria of becoming a deity and existing on a supernatural plane. A degree of control enters in that these violent seizures can be terminated by aspersions with holy water (Bastide 1960: 258). This control is, however, purely negative, and in no way determines the form of the possession.

There is no initiation. It is replaced by the free choice of the spirits or 'enchantés' who choose whomever they want for devotees (or are chosen by whomever wants them). Both men and women are possessed. In the first possession the enchanté is savage. The devotee must wait a year before the enchanté manifests his personaiity, receives a name, and enters into the framework of mythology. He is then considered civilized, that is, possession is more regulated and less fearful (Bastide 1960: 258-259).

The Catimbó then is a cult that became disorganized partially as a result of syncretism, which multiplied the number of spirits and mixed the tenets and practices of very different religions. Also, because the members of the cult are very poor and can not afford initiations, individuals, rather than learning how to fit their personality traits into the already established pattern of an existing prototype, invent a spirit conforming to their own personal needs. It is interesting to note that because the Catimbó is still very much a community phenomenon it seems to be increasing in its degree of organization. The spirits belonging to the individual members are being fitted into a mythology, and perhaps, as more characteristics are attributed to them, their number and personality traits will stabilize and they will be passed on in patterned form. New devotees will then perhaps be possessed by already invented and characterized enchantés rather than inventing their own. This, of course, perhaps may not be the case. Bastide does not indicate how coherent the mythology is. Perhaps the cult will continue with each person inventing his own spirit, with no development of social control in the form of determined patterns of behavior when possessed.

It seems to be in the Brazilian urban centers, where many conflicting forces come into play, that the cults really approach the pole of individualism, pathology, and magic, as evidenced by the Macumba in Rio de Janeiro and especially in São Paulo. The urban Macumba is too integrated into the Brazilian milieu to maintain the essence of African tradition as many Candomblés have managed to do. This is because of demographic and historical reasons. The largest congregation of people of African descent is in urban Bahia where the Candomblés have remained most traditional. The Macumba is no longer controlled by a structured collective memory because its members do not constitute an integrated community as is more so the case in Bahia. It has therefore become quite individualized. New deities are fabricated to correspond to personifications of the profound impulses and anxieties of the devotees, thus possession, since it merely expresses individual libidos, tends to be hysterical. There is no mythology to regulate the trance and make it an imitation of divine models (Bastide 1960: 406-409, 526).

In Rio the devotees or mediums become possessed as in the other cults, but in São Paulo the Macumba has reached an extreme in that it is no longer religion but magic. The economic and social insecurity of this urban center, in which there is very little traditional African heritage, pushes this metamorphosis from religion to magic. The need for medical help, for example, forces the priest to become a healer, and the cult becomes a simple consultation of the spirits through him (Bastide 1960: 408, 413, 421). Also there exists another cult, the Umbanda, a modern, syncretistic organization composed of European, Indian, and African elements rather than a traditional cult of African origin, and thus not within the scope of this paper. The Umbanda is a more sophisticated possession cult which has taken over the elements of the Macumba that fit its bourgeois orientation and consequently attracts the upwardly aspiring former Macumba members. Thus the Macumba, particularly in São Paulo, is left as a purely magic cult (Bastide 1944-1945).

The macumbeiro is frequently a person who was ill and who, upon being cured by another macumbeiro, became a servant of the spirits. He learns herbs and prayers and goes into trances during which people can consult his spirits. His trance is not controlled by any social group. It is completely individualistic and reflects only his personal libido (Bastide 1960: 406-409). It seems that a macumbeiro would be more likely to be neurotic than would the ordinary member of a traditional possession cult because whereas the former is expressing his personal libido in a non-socially controlled manner, the latter must express his in conformity with stringent social regulations. Douyon's information on Haiti also shows clearly the relationship between social disorganization and individual disorganization, although he concentrates only on the element of individual disorganization and ignores the element of culture change.[1]

---

[1] As might well be expected, fraudulent possessions, rare in traditional cults because beliefs were stronger and because there were tests to verify whether or not the trance was sincere, are more prevalent in disorganized cults. Bastide links them to the penetration of whites into the African cults in Brazil and to the development of tourism (1950: 251). Landes also notes that the members of the non-traditional Candomblé de Caboclo (African mixed with Indian elements) seem to have too much control over their deities to be really possessed. They can turn their trances off and on at will, and appear much less honest than the traditional Yoruba women (1947: 168-169). Dr. Jean-Baptiste Romain, chairman of the Anthropology Department at the University of Haiti informed me in a private conversation that touristic Vodun ceremonies can be set up at the drop of a hat — containing American dollars, of course. This type performance can not be serious, and is detrimental to the traditional religious structure. In Brazil, possession cults of African origin are on the traditional tourist circuit.

CHAPTER TEN

PHILOSOPHICAL IMPLICATIONS OF POSSESSION

As Durkheim saw religious forms as a reflection of social structural elements, Bastide, on the contrary, proceeds from the religious sphere to the social. The society is structured according to the collective representations determined by the norms of the religious system of the community (Bastide 1960: 521). Thus the human community is an imitation of the divine, and men are symbols of their gods not only while possessed by them but also when leading their normal lives. Thus the gods are the foundation of the real existence of man because they embody the significant meanings of life on their sacred level (Duvignand 1959: 257).

The ritual of possession is thus a repetition; man's acting out in the present what the gods made real in the beginning of time. Man's reflection of the gods in possession ceremonies is not just a game of mirrors, however, but is related to a more profound reality. It is not just a repetition of archaic gestures, but is a lived reality because the possessed person becomes his deity on ritual occasions. Before possession he imitated mythical events, whereas when he becomes possessed he relives these same events. He also participates in the deity's character because he has some of the deity mystically inculcated into him. In some places a hole is actually made in the devotee's head where the deity, or some aspect of him, is considered to reside. Thus in possession ceremonies the possessed become the deities and act out their myths. Their trances interact and the participants respond to a reality in which the visions and stimuli are from the mystical world. Several trances come together complementarily forming an ensemble of adequate stimuli and responses corresponding to the scenario imposed by the mythical tradition (Bastide 1958: 173-174, 177, 211).

"Ainsi le corps de ballet, son orchestre et son décor reproduisent les lieux et les acteurs des origines". (Thus the ballet troupe, its orchestra and its decor reproduce the places and the actors of the beginnings — author's translation) (Griaule 1966: 178). In the Candomblé ceremony the world is recreated. In the temple the ground is the earth, the ceiling the sky, and the central pillar (poteau mitan down which the Loa slide in Haiti) is the phallus symbolizing the eternal recreation of life by the sexual union of earth and sky, woman and man. The dance of the deities mimes the elements of nature. In Bahia, Shango is the god of thunder and lightening, Yansan of storms, Oshun of rivers, etc., as in the Yoruba pantheon in Nigeria. There are equivalents in the other pantheons also. Thus the temple is the world reconstituted in its mystical reality, the true reality (Bastide 1958: 72).

"La danse, est, pour le Négro-Africain, le moyen le plus naturel d'exprimer une idée; une émotion. Que l'émotion le saississe — joie ou tristesse, gratitude ou indignation — le Négro-Africain danse" (The dance is for the Black African the most natural means of expressing an idea; an emotion. Whatever emotion may seize him — joy or sadness, gratitude or indignation — the black African dances — author's translation) (Mars 1966: 24-25). "La danse à l'origine—il en est encore ainsi en Afrique Noire—est langage, le langage le plus complet", (The dance in the beginning — it is still true in Black Africa — is language, the most complete language — author's translation) — Léopold Sédar Senghor (Mars 1966: 25).

Thus the dance for Africans and their New World descendents puts their whole bodies into play and gets close to the source of emotion, expressing it in dramatic language. The ecstatic dance of the possessed is full of significance. It contains information and has a semantic structure. Its vocabulary is the mythological characters of the deities, its syntax the rapport between them: their genealogies, marriages, and disputes. The individual ecstasies dialogue among themselves, forming a language written in choreographed gestures (Mars 1966: 24-25).

According to Bastide, there are two manners in which men can represent the supernatural beings. They can don masks and act out the roles of the deities, never totally forgetting that they have not actually become the deities, with wise spectators sharing this recognition. In the other form of representation the man who incarnates the living god (homem-do-deus-vivo) does not don a mask, but his physiognomy changes to simulate that of the god. In the first case the garb makes the god. In the second the man first becomes the god, then dons the appropriate costume. "In the first case religion approaches the theater; in the second case there is a metamorphosis of the personality" (Bastide 1953: 49-50—author's translation).

What characterizes a religion, whatever kind it may be, is the establishment of a contact between the world of men and the world of the sacred, that of the gods and supernatural forces. But if in Western religions it is man who, with difficulty, through a usually painful effort, manages to elevate himself to God, in the so-called primitive religions it is the deities who descend and come for a few minutes to inhabit the bodies of their faithful ones. The nucleus of Afro-Brazilian religions [and other African and Afro-American religions in question] is, then, this entrance of the Orisha into the organism, into the head, into the muscles; it is the 'fall of the saints' come from ancestral Africa to the sanctuaries of Bahia or Pernambuco (Bastide 1953: 29—author's translation).

Thus in possession the frontiers between natural and supernatural no longer exist. Ecstasy has made the desired communion a reality (Bastide 1958: 22). The human and the divine intersect, and man transcends his humanity. Also individuals transcend their specific human roles in becoming someone more powerful than themselves (Duvignand 1959: 256, 258). In addition, the entire community of deracinated Africans affirms, in possession by deities who come from Africa for the occasion, its awareness of its historical origins and its belief in the continuing existence of the mythical community of the ancestors (Duvignand 1959: 255; Verger 1954: 336).

Possession is the supreme religious act, but it is in essence extremely human and related to the basic, everyday concerns of human life, although transposed to a sacred plane. Though human reality is abolished and action takes place on a more meaningful, supernatural plane, the deities have grossly human characteristics. They are happy while singing, dancing, and eating in the bodies of their devotees. They embody the qualities and faults, anxieties, hopes, wishes, and needs of man; everything meaningful in his life. He projects images of what he is, needs, and wants onto the personalities and myths of the deities, and then embodies them in possession and acts them out. In the Zar cult, among the Songhay, and in Haiti, the deities are so much a part of everyday life that they are assigned historical roles. In Haiti, for example, Mars reports that certain Loa supposedly took part in the war for independence, and the emperor and fierce revolutionary Jean-Jacques Dessalines is now a Loa (1948: 1082).

In Bahia, a person is considered to manifest various degrees in a hierarchy of 'being' depending upon the closeness and quality of his rapport with the supernatural. Existence is related to power and all power comes from the gods. Various rituals cause the individual to participate more and more in the nature and force of the Orisha, permitting him to acquire more and more being. This augmentation of being is manifest externally in luck, prosperity, health, etc. Among the Yoruba and their descendants in the New World, luck is not an impersonal quality, the result of chance or fortuitous circumstances, but is linked to the gods. Luck is a divine benediction indicating participation in the world of the divine beings (Bastide 1958: 212).

Evil is, of course, the contrary, or decrease in being, outwardly manifest in illness, unhappiness, failure, etc. This occurs because a devotee violates a taboo, neglects ritual obligations, or sometimes his degree of being is worn away by the passage of time. He must therefore perform a washing of the head, collar, or pearls (concrete symbols of his deity which embody some of the deity's strength) ceremony to renew his power, and must especially perform such a ceremony in time of trouble, since this is when he most needs strong links with the supernatural. The washing ceremony re-establishes the deity in the head of the devotee by the use of herbal substances imbued with the power of the supernatural partner. "Man's is not a simple imitation, or a simple repetition of the being of the Orisha, but it is a real divination, the branching of man on the divine trunk" (Bastide 1958: 213 — author's translation).

The social hierarchy of the Candomblé therefore, is manifest outwardly by an individual's degree of power, command, and authority over those of lower ritual status, but this authority is merely a radiation of his being, or the degree of being the Orisha has in him (Bastide 1958: 213). The same is true in the Zar cult. Members are hierarchically grouped in a brotherhood around the leader or healer, who is the most experienced. The hierarchy within the brotherhood corresponds to the hierarchy of the Zar of the members (Leiris 1958: 19). Occupants of some roles in the Candomblé, such as that of attendant (ekedi), can not increase their degree of being because they do not get possessed, hence their social position does not change. They participate in few rituals other than as attendants, thus can not fortify their links with the Orisha.

The high priests and priestesses are the highest authorities in the religious hierarchy because of their constant and intimate participation in and communication with the divine world. They have achieved the highest degree of existence. This close rapport explains why they can control their deities, rather than be controlled by them. Respect due them and others does not go to the person per se, but through him to his principal deity, the Orisha to whom he belongs. This Orisha actually deserves anything directed to the person because the Orisha make individual lives what they are (Bastide 1958: 213).

Within the Candomblé, power struggles are translated as struggles between the gods, and two people are not expected to get along if there is a traditional enmity between their deities. An analogous situation probably obtains in the other societies also. If the deities of the interested individuals are related, such power struggles may be seen as small family spats. A myth in a particular Candomblé may also change on the basis of what actually happens between people, since the structure of the natural and supernatural planes must remain consistent. When traditional, orthodox African myths do not fit the social realities, they are changed (Bastide 1958: 229). Of course this is probably not actually done consciously, but is rather a gradual process.

The history of men is introduced into the metaphysics, and with this human history, all of the contingencies of political struggles, clan battles, and priestly ambitions. The Orisha, in addition to being gods of nature and compartments of reality, are also ancestors of competing clans and lineages, as reflected in the myths. Thus the proliferation of myths is linked to the events and hazards of history. The mythology is composed of superimposed strata, the chronology of which reflects historical transformations recorded according to traditional form (Bastide 1958: 231). Human history is thus divinized and given greater significance because it is relived as if it were the actions of the gods.

Hence the possession ritual expresses the ultimate meaning of man's life in exhibiting his divine nature. It also causes a transformation in his social and psychological state because through ritual participation man increases his degree of being, manifest in psychological and social well-being. In the ritual he affirms the ultimate values of his community and recapitulates man's relationship to the ancestors, to history, to nature, and to the contemporary scene. He emerges from participation in a ritual with a strengthened and freshened sense of his rapport with the cosmos, the society, and himself. A man so integrated is likely to function more effectively in life than one whose adjustment is tenuous or weakening, and this is reflected in the relative success of his undertakings. Hence the ritual participant is internally changed by the ritual in which he has participated, and his external world changes accordingly.

CHAPTER ELEVEN

THE NORMALITY
OR ABNORMALITY OF POSSESSION

The phenomenon of possession was seen in the past as a hysterical manifestation. Dorsainvil, in his 1912 study of Haitian Vodun classified possession as a kind of neurosis resulting in part from a historical tradition which makes such seizures respectable, and in part from the inheritance of neurotic tendencies within the family of the possessed (Wittkower 1964: 76-77). Possession has much in common with hypnotic states, epilepsy, and hysteria. Like epilepsy there is frequently an aura, retrograde amnesia for the period, and sometimes convulsions, though the latter, if they occur, come only during ceremonies. The usual concomitant features and aftereffects of an epileptic attack are missing (Wittkower 1964: 77). However, unlike epilepsy, possession is provoked and terminated by culturally defined cues on specific ritual occasions.

Wittkower insists that possession should not be equated with hysteria, as is most frequently done, because hysteria is a disease of prolonged duration whereas possession is a short-term manifestation after which the individual recovers his normal personality. Possession has some of the features of a neurotic episode, and it is possible that in hysterical individuals the possession state may be a manifestation of this neurosis or of the psychosis of a psychotic. In most of the religions in question experienced priests can supposedly distinguish between ceremonial and neurotic or psychotic possession (1964: 77). The relationship between possession and hypnotic states has already been treated at length.

Experiments in France have indicated that groups can collectively experience possession similar to the Haitian form (and, analogously, to that of the other groups in question), and seizures like possession can be stimulated by sonic driving. Thus, considering the variety of physical, physiological, bio-chemical, and neuro-dynamic factors which may provoke possession, it becomes apparent that possession is not a distinct clinical entity, but an ensemble of manifestations arising in pathological as well as normal psyches (Douyon 1964: 80-81).

According to Wallace, "Despite equivalence of process, that which is regarded as 'illness' in one society may be regarded as merely one aspect of the normal and healthy life in another" (1966: 165). For Benedict, the normal is behavior that is both elaborated and expected by a particular society; the abnormal, that which is not accepted. Some societies may approve highly unstable behavior, such as a proclivity for trance states, and not make demands with which such people can not cope, thus classing them as normal members of the society (1934: 72-75). Herskovits insists that possession is a normal phenomenon because it is set in a cultural mold like all phases of conventional living. Also it happens to numerous very different kinds of people in a regular and disciplined fashion and is accepted as a normal phenomenon by the members of the society (Herkovits 1966: 359; Verger 1954: 327).

In many societies, religious ritual and other elements of ceremonial protocol require individuals of certain statuses to undergo types of experiences which in contemporary Western psychiatric tradition are regarded as symptomatic of mental disorder. This class of pseudo-illnesses, culturally enjoined, includes such diverse phenomena as ritual dissociation (trance and possession), drug or alcoholic intoxication (as, for example, in the Native American Church where the Indians have the taking of peyote as a sacrament), self-mortification leading to hallucinations (as in the Plains Indians' vision quest), ceremonial torture and cannibalism, and ecstatic conversion experiences. The physiological and psychological mechanisms immediately involved in the 'abnormal' state in such pseudo-disorders may well be the same as those involved in symptom production in Western mental patients. Nevertheless, the consequences of such experiences are vastly different, since a 'ceremonial' neurosis or psychosis, unlike the 'true' disease, is voluntarily initiated, is usually reversible, and leads neither the subject nor his associates to classify him as abnormal and unworthy of complete social participation. Such disorders are comparable, in Western society, to the generation of dissociated states in healthy individuals by hypnosis, or the production of hallucinations by administration of LSD [1] or sensory deprivation, or the elicitation of disorganized speech in guests at a cocktail party. The subjects of such manifestations are not classified as mentally ill despite the fact that under special circumstances they have temporarily entered states

[1] As has been noted, when a Haitian mambo was given LSD, her response was about the same as in possession.

which chronically characterize some mentally ill persons (Wallace 1966: 181-182).

Spiro considers that there are two pan-human criteria of behavioral pathology or normality: adaptiveness and optimum functioning within the society. Any condition, organic or behavioral, which produces their opposite, is pathological. Thus if the religious beliefs or rituals are maladaptive and/or reduce optimum functioning, the behavior provoked by them is abnormal. Although these criteria for judging behavior are universally applicable, it does not follow that all instances of phenotypically similar behavior or beliefs, when evaluated by these criteria, will lead to the same judgements because the judgements must be relative to the socio-cultural context in which the behavior occurs. Each culture constructs its own reality in relation to which behavior is normal or distorted. Thus two very similar acts could be judged totally differently in different socio-cultural contexts (1965: 105).

Thus Spiro, like Wallace, concludes that religious behavior in some other societies, though similar to that which characterizes abnormal individuals in Western society, is not necessarily, or even usually, abnormal when sanctioned or prescribed by the society and taught to the actors as part of their cultural heritage, through the usual techniques of instruction and imitation. Therefore such beliefs and behavior are expressions, rather than distortions, of the culturally constituted reality of these societies. They are consistent with, rather than obstacles to, social and cultural functioning (Spiro 1965: 105).

Psychotic beliefs and behavior are devised by the actor to try to reduce painful tension caused by inner conflicts based on private distortions of the cultural reality, and result in impaired socio-cultural functioning. Religious behavioral manifestations, though not devised by the actors to reduce such conflicts, may be used to that end. As culturally constituted defenses they are consistent with, rather than distortions of, reality, are culturally sanctioned rather than prohibited, and protect the individual and the society from the disruptive consequences of the acting out of shameful and/or forbidden needs and private defensive maneuvers (Spiro 1965: 105).

According to Spiro, the behavior of Burmese Buddhist monks is phenotypically similar to that of schizoids [1] or schizophrenics, as

---

[1] According to Bateson and Mead, ordinary personal adjustment in Balinese culture approximates in form the kind of maladjustment which in a Western cultural setting would be considered schizoid. In this context the trance is a cultural form accessible to

would indicate Rorschach analyses of such monks without consideration of the cultural context. Left to their own resources many would probably become genuine psychotics. However, the religion provides a culturally constituted fantasy and action system which they can use to resolve their own inner conflicts and thus avoid the pathological behavior which might otherwise result. Demands are not made on them with which they can not cope (Spiro 1965: 107-108).

Rorschach protocols of the Burmese Buddhist monks are similar to those of Burmese laymen, differing only in degree. The monks have more of the same problems which face the average Burmese male (Spiro 1965: 107-108). Their conflicts lie in what Devereux would term the ethnic, as opposed to individual unconscious — that portion of the total unconscious segment of the individual's psyche which most members of the cultural community have in common. The culture provides ways of implementing these ethnic neuroses, this being the factor which differentiates them from private neuroses for which the symptoms are idiosyncratically evolved. The culture places usually ritualized devices at the disposal of those individuals whose conflicts are conventional within the community (1956: 25, 30).

Thus the Burmese Buddhist monks have powerful cultural resources for the solution of their problems in the institution of monastic life. The roles provided satisfy their prohibited or shameful needs and relieve their fears and anxieties. Such potentially disruptive psychic variables, instead of provoking socially and individually disruptive behavior, provide the motivational basis for the persistence of the most highly valued institution in Burmese society — monasticism. This institution provides for the resolution of the inner conflicts of the Burmese males involved by allowing them to gratify drives and reduce anxieties in a disguised, and hence socially acceptable manner, precluding pathological behavior. The monk is

---

most Balinese, occurring in different proportions in different villages (1942: xvi, 35). However, habitual trancers may discontinue their practice of falling into trances for diverse reasons and continue to lead a normal life, e.g., little girl trance dancers stop at menarche but none of the authors indicate whether or not these girls are particularly prone to becoming adult trancers; and some people cease trancing because it leaves them too physically exhausted or because they move to another village. Psychological tests given to strong trancers and to a control group not characterized by trances showed no difference between the personality structures of the two groups (Belo 1960: 10). Thus the trance in Bali does not seem to be the special property of any special personality type, but rather a relatively universal product of the socialization process and the cultural values which determine it.

protected from mental illness; the society is protected from the disruptive influence of antisocial behavior; and a key institution is provided with a powerful motivational basis (Spiro 1965: 108-109).

There are significant differences in the monastic and psychotic resolutions of similar problems. Initially there are some differences in the genesis of the conflict. The conflict of the monk is located in modal features of the society, whereas that of the psychotic may not be. The monk's conflict is more intense than that of the normal Burmese male, and that of the psychotic is yet more intense, to the point of making him unable to perceive reality in the culturally determined way, or to take advantage of the institutionalized defense mechanisms it provides. The psychotic is thus seen as abnormal by his fellows, whereas the monk, whose private world view corresponds to the public world view of the society, expresses in his behavior the values most cherished in Burmese culture (Spiro 1965: 109-111).

Spiro concludes that in most traditional areas where religious beliefs and practices continue to carry conviction, religion is the cultural system par excellence by means of which conflict resolution is achieved. The religion provides highly efficient, culturally constituted defense mechanisms. Abnormal behavior can be expected to appear (1965: 111-113):

— When emotional conflict is idiosyncratic so cultural means are not available as a potential basis for culturally constituted defense mechanisms.
— When emotional conflict is modal and cultural means are available for conflict resolution, but these means are inadequately taught or learned.
— When under conditions of rapid social change culturally constituted defense mechanisms are unavailable because old institutions have been discarded or because the new situation creates a new set of conflicts.

Any of these three conditions is propitious to, but not necessarily sufficient for the production of abnormal behavior. Although the emotional conflict is potentially pathogenic it need not produce pathology. Emotional conflict issues in pathology only if it is not resolved or if it is resolved in a manner characterized by psychic distortion and/or socio-cultural impairment, which is then termed neurotic or psychotic (Spiro 1965: 111-113). These three factors have been discussed previously in relationship to both mental illness and social change.

Haitian psychiatrist Emerson Douyon did a psychological study of members of the Vodun religion in Port-au-Prince using Rorschach and Sacks tests among others, plus autobiographies and observation of the participants' behavior. No tests were done during the trance period. His intent was to ascertain if there is a characteristic profile of the personalities of the people subject to possession, and if so if it is (1964: 2, 5):

— Normal, i.e., conforming exclusively to the collective religious and cultural values which are socially accepted and universally distributed within the homogeneous ethnic community.
— Characterological — relative to a particular receptivity to hypnotic conditioning or because of a hereditary predisposition to it.
— A well-defined pathological condition, and if so is it organic, neurotic or psychotic.

Douyon wanted to discover if there are significant differences between those who are possessed only during ceremonies and those who are possessed on non-ceremonial occasions. Also are there significant differences between people who become possessed and those who never do? If so do these differences reveal particular traits which would classify the possessed person as pathological or simply as easily conditioned to a cultural complex? He was also concerned with the positive or negative functional significance of possession for the personalities of those prone to this state (1964: 4; 1965: 156).

Douyon initially wanted to have an experimental group divided into two parts — those who were only ceremonially possessed and those who were only possessed on non-ceremonial occasions. The control group was to be divided between Catholics who were not involved with Vodun and people involved with Vodun who did not become possessed. He could find few Catholics who were totally uninvolved with Vodun in the chosen social milieu, and they, being uninvolved for very diverse reasons, did not form a homogeneous group. The ceremonial—non-ceremonial dichotomy proved artificial. Any person who became possessed could do so in or outside of the ceremonial atmosphere. People who were more frequently possessed in one setting or the other did not differ in behavior or degree of psychopathology. Men were eliminated from the experiment because very few men ever got possessed and those who did were, according to informants, alcoholics or degenerates, supposedly because they had Loa who treated them badly. Most men who could go into trances became houngans, who were difficult to work with because of their dramatic, exploitative, arrogant attitudes (Douyon 1964: 1-6, 118-120, 224).

His forty-four subjects, twenty-five experimental, who became possessed, and nineteen control, who did not, were unmarried, illiterate Catholic women of peasant origins who were domestics in or close to Port-au-Prince, and were between the ages of twenty and forty. The similarity of social standing and occupation was to facilitate the comparison. These were all women presumed normal by other members of their society, and whose physical states tested as normal. All people whose possessions were obviously associated with mental, nervous, or physical illness, or whose personalities and conduct made them suspect in their own milieu were eliminated. To establish criteria for the normal Haitian peasant personality, Douyon tested a sample of both men and women (1964: 99, 101-102, 121, 156). It would seem that the presence of men in this normal base would be detrimental to the validity of the results of the study since all of the people in the experiment were women, and their normality was measured against the personalities of both men and women. Since only female experimenters were used, Douyon should have derived the normal personality base from a wholly female sample.

The psychological tests were used in conjunction with autobiographical information about the subjects, and noticeable correlations were found between psychological realities and their past and present behavior. The childhoods and family backgrounds of the control and experimental groups were similar, members of the same families being in both groups, although their adult lives were different. Most of the subjects considered their poverty to be the main source of all the problems of their lives. Most felt rejected by their families, many having been sent away from home at a young age to do domestic service. There was frequently a strong attachment to the maternal image and feeling of having been the mother's preferred child, contrasted with a marked aversion for a brutal father. Most were very suspicious toward others, and therefore had poor relationships with other people of both sexes, sometimes becoming involved in violent disputes, even to the point of going to prison. Unmarried themselves the women in the experimental group envied married women, and many were prostitutes and/or lesbians. Members of the control group tended to be concubines, but less promiscuous and had a more ordered love life. All of the women, with the experimental group being more extreme, were characterized by a clear nostalgia for their childhood, the period of greatest happiness (as was predicted in the chapter on socialization), and great pessimism for the future, which promised nothing good, only death. They were depressed because of their constant fear of others and because they saw their state of social and economic misery as unchangeable, which was pretty much a correct appraisal of reality. Some considered suicide in periods of despair, but had obviously not killed themselves though they might be masochistic in their trances.

All grew up in a world peopled by danger and evil beings such as loupgarous (werewolves) and bakas, and had nightmares about them, which colored their perceptions of other people. They were threatened by their parents with punishment by such beings in addition to the actual physical punishment that was part of the traditional child-rearing practice. They were also characterized by definite submission and obedience to authority figures, with only the Loa being depended upon in times of need.

The women in the experimental group remembered observing their mothers' possessions, feeling that they, as favorites, would inherit this ability. The families of these women who became possessed also had many cases of alcoholic or 'nervous' individuals and marginal or 'bizarre' relatives. Thus they seemed to have inherited affective constitutions having a natural disposition for a whole gamut of nervous manifestations (Douyon 1964: 93, 139, 206-215; 1965: 157-158).

Douyon found no physical or neurological differences between the experimental and control groups. In some areas the control group was a bit healthier. There were no elements systematically present or absent in either group in the laboratory tests. The experimental group was not mentally weaker than other people from the same milieu, and their approach to reality was as concrete in Haitian terms as everyone else's. Both groups had the same supernatural beliefs.

The Rorschach results revealed identical general profiles for both groups but detailed analysis revealed significant differences. Members of the control group tended to have what Douyon refers to as 'poor', rigid personalities characterized by strongly defensive reactions and stereotyping of thoughts and responses. The group of women prone to possession tended to have personalities he classifies as inadequate, perturbed, i.e., aggressive, autistic, with confused logic; or very perturbed, i.e., they responded with automatic phrases, were purely autistic, and responded arbitrarily to stimuli. Most women in the experimental group fell into the inadequate and perturbed categories. Members of this group were characterized by high degrees of anxiety, frequently reflective of past traumas and the expectation of future ones, and definite deficiencies in the control of their impulses, showing great instability of moods and outbursts of great affect (Douyon 1964: 128, 133, 138, 182, 187, 191, 195, 197, 214-215; 1965: 157; 1968: 116-117).

Stainbrook found that in Bahia women associated with the Candomblé who did not become possessed often exhibited unusual anxiety or definite hostility or stubbornness. He did not, however, mention any specifics concerning the personalities of the women who became possessed except that if they were very neurotic or psychotic they could not mold themselves to the demands of the Candomblé (1952: 334). It seems reasonable that the rigid, defended personality could not let down its defenses to allow other facets of the personality, normally repressed, to come to the fore during possession. The anxiety and hostility are probably a result of the fact that such drives are not being expressed but are repressed although the culture provides a vehicle for their expression. The experimental group releases their strong feelings in possession and compensates for the unhappy elements of their lives.

Douyon concludes then that women who become possessed have a personality structure, clearly different from that of the normal Haitian peasant, which he would consider neurotic in some cases and psychotic in others. Also they belong to families in which other people are also possessed, and they inherit both the Loa and the psychological predisposition to become possessed. Possession is not limited, however, to specific personality types. The individuals involved may be hysterical, depressive, or schizophrenic, their seizures going from mild neurotic reactions to clearly psychotic delirium. Possession, according to Douyon, is an infantile reaction requiring, in addition to specific conditioning experiences, a disturbed, anxious, and depressed personality. Thus, one must be psychologically troubled to go into a trance or be possessed (Douyon 1964: 158, 198, 216; 1968: 117-118; 1967: 5). This conclusion seems to contradict the fact that possession-like states can be induced by sonic driving, as Douyon recognizes, in people who are not neurotic or psychotic. It is not consistent either with Douyon's mention of experimentally induced group possession in France, unless he would also consider all of these people neurotic or psychotic, and he gives no indication that this is the case.

People subject to possession are clearly trying to escape from reality and also tend to do so in other ways under stressful conditions. Sixty-four per cent of Douyon's experimental group tended to lose consciousness during arguments, after deceptions, or at the death of a relative, friend, or neighbor. Such seizures differ from ceremonial possession in that no new personality is taken on, and there is no ideation. These seizures may be similar to epileptic attacks, but are not symptomatic of epilepsy. The relationship of ceremonial possession to such states emphasizes the subject's proclivity for mental dissociation as a method of escape from reality when she is unable to face a difficult or upsetting situation in a normal manner. This is analogous to the tendency to go to sleep under stressful conditions characteristic of the Balinese. The individual may escape from any stressful situation by having a seizure, the type being dependent upon the context and content of the stress.[1]

Funeral seizures, angry seizures, and ceremonial seizures seem to be different expressions of the same intolerance of frustration and the same rage at one's powerlessness before adversity (Douyon 1964: 238-239; 1965: 158-159). The chapter on the socialization process establishes that Haitian peasants tend to grow up with low frustration tolerance levels coupled with much repressed hostility against authority figures.

It would seem from the information on socialization in Haiti that the people liable to possession are, like Spiro's Burmese Buddhist monks, like everyone else but even more so. This is substantiated by Douyon's remark that any Haitian peasant may potentially experience possession-like seizures in situations of great stress. The loss of a loved one or violent anger is often enough to provoke an explosion of affect, the uncontrollable character of which reproduces in part the clinical tableau of the trance state (1964: 80-81). The outline of the typical socialization pattern of the Haitian peasants is quite similar to that reported for the women in the experiment except that elements in the lives of the members of the experimental group seem exaggerated. Thus their problems are located in the ethnic unconscious rather than the private one and they can take advantage of the cultural mechanisms available for the resolution of the problems the culture creates. Their conflicts are apparently consistent with the general behavioral tendencies and world view of their

---

[1] The same, of course, was true with Victorian ladies, who could faint in any situation with which they could not cope.

compatriots. Also, as with the Burmese monks, the acting out of their fantasies by the people who become possessed is the mainstay of the whole religious system.

Possession as described by the women involved appears to be essentially provoked from the outside. The subjects report not being able to see another person go into possession without doing so themselves. Except for those that occur during sleep, possessions are always public, or quickly become so as people come to hear the words of the Loa. The possessed person feels the need to interact with others during the trance and usually feels that her Loa is welcomed by the spectators. She receives gifts and feels protected by all, enjoying the attention she receives. However, though the subjects say they can not be possessed at will, they can invoke the Loa, who may possess their devotees if they wish (Douyon 1964: 159, 239). Also, from other accounts it is evident that some devotees, particularly priestesses, can indeed be possessed at will, although it is not certain that they can determine which deity or deities will come (Bourguignon 1965; Huxley 1966: passim).

Despite this attitude toward the external provocation of possession, it is apparent that it is actually to a great extent provoked by the initiative of the devotee, who may inhibit or favor the arrival of the deity. Thus most, if not all, possessions are partially responses to unconscious or conscious desires, as has been emphasized in the chapters on neurophysiology and hypnosis.

Douyon thus insists that possession is explainable less by the Vodun cult than by the personalities of the individuals who become possessed. He sees possession as a complex psychophysiological response to essentially endogenous stimulation, even among people who seem mainly influenced by the climate of the ceremony. The ceremony is an excuse, but is not indispensable. It is not the only occasion or pretext for mental decomposition, and possession may have only a distant rapport with the actual religion. Thus the behavior of the women who become possessed clearly reflects an abnormal personality, with the whole gamut of nervous symptoms: splitting of the personality, loss of contact with reality, regression, delusions and hallucinations, aggression, amnesia, confusion, affective dramatization, etc. (Douyon 1964: 5-7, 249).

Douyon begins by saying that in evaluating the phenomenon of possession the cultural context must be considered, yet in analysing the behavior of the women who become possessed he does not actually take it into consideration. Most of the nervous symptoms he describes are behavioral elements consistent with the world view of the average Haitian peasant. The Loa exist and they possess people, filling the person's body with their own personality and type of affect. The lack of contact with reality, delusions, hallucinations, and confusion are only such in relationship to the profane reality, but in the possession situation an entirely new reality is created, which is also consistent with the community world view. It is not fair to say that the ceremonies are merely an excuse for mental decomposition or that possession may have only a distant rapport with the religion because to do so is to willfully ignore the content of the religious beliefs and their all-pervasive influence in Haitian peasant life. Non-ceremonial possession, although not provoked by the stimuli present in the ritual, is considered by folk theory to be the same religiously inspired and patterned phenomenon, following a definite, acceptable model constructed by the culture.

Thus, although the people who become possessed may have psychological problems, which I contend are mainly part of the ethnic unconscious and merely exaggerated versions of the psychological make-up of other Haitian peasant women, these problems must be understood in terms of the world view of the community. Douyon proposes to do this but does not, probably mainly because of his psychiatric orientation. He ignores cultural definitions and attitudes to look at the 'harder' data of psychological test results, 'objective' observation of actual behavior, and concrete social and economic facts. He does not deal with the cultural beliefs which supply the meaning and content for his hard data, thus I think his conclusions are exaggerated. Also, in choosing his subjects he explicitly says that he is choosing people deemed normal and socially adjusted by others in their milieu, rejecting anyone considered maladjusted. The behavior they exhibit which, although it may 'objectively', that is in terms of Western middle class values, appear inspired by abnormal or neurotic motivation, is, in their lower class Haitian milieu, apparently quite acceptable and expected. Also the state of possession is not as entirely psychogenic as Douyon states, as was indicated in the chapter on neurophysiology.

Douyon characterizes his control group, the normal people, as having 'poor' personalities, but 'poor' in relation to whom, since these are the people against whom he is supposedly judging the women who become possessed. Are they poor in relation to the initial sample he tested to find a basis for evaluation, or poor in an absolute sense as defined by the psychological tests without reference to the culture? If the former, his standard of judgement is not really accurate since there were men in the original sample and none in the control group, and if the latter, the fallacies are obvious. Are the members of the experimental group inadequate and perturbed only in relationship to the rigid, extremely defensive control group women, or to the original test group? Neither Douyon nor any of the other authors I have read mentions the folk attitude toward this distinction between people who do and do not become possessed. All the people Douyon tested were considered normal in their milieu. It is never clear which group is more normal in terms of general Haitian peasant expectations, those who become possessed or those who do not. All the groups under consideration distinguish normal religious manifestations from phenotypically similar manifestations of insanity. Given the important religious significance, plus the social and psychological advantages accruing to the people who become possessed, it would seem that they would be considered normal, and be respected and envied because their ability brings them prestige and power in the peasant social structure and their behavior during possession is beneficial to the whole community because man is communicating with the gods.

According to Douyon, three factors concur to produce possession (1964: 248):

— Transmission of pathological attitudes within the family.
— A milieu propitious to conditioning to trance behavior and identification with people who become possessed.
— The presence of at least one spectator to give a sense to the possession and to respond to the possessed person.

These factors are by no means exhaustive. I would agree that there are both neurophysiological and psychosocial propensities to possession transmitted within the family, but not that they are necessarily pathological. All members of Douyon's experimental group came from a background of people prone to possession, particularly on the matrilinear side. They participated in ceremonies, even if uninitiated, and looked forward to being possessed for the benefits which would accrue to them. Members of the control group were indifferent or hostile to the idea of possession (Douyon 1964: 237, 241, 243).

It is not clear whether this attitude on the part of the members of the control group reflects individual psychological or socio-cultural elements. People striving for or aspiring to upward mobility in the society would tend to have such indifferent or hostile attitudes toward the possession state because they would regard it as an element of the lower class peasant culture from which they are trying to escape. It is thus possible that the reason for this difference in attitude, as well as the rigidity of the personalities of the members of the control group, is their desire for upward mobility. It could also be the rigidity and defensiveness of their personalities which cause these women to be indifferent or hostile to possession.

This is an important element to consider, although Douyon does not, because all of the women tested are of peasant origins and work as domestics for relatively affluent families in an urban center. They are deracinated from their peasant origins and the internally coherent social and cultural systems that were a part of the rural community. In the city Vodun and possession are negatively valued by educated and aspiring people, not positively valued as in the peasant communities. In the rural areas families were better organized, and people were not abandoned or at loose ends. Much of the disturbed quality of the personalities of the women in Douyon's experiment is very likely a result of the deracinated situation in which these women find themselves, feeling abandoned by their families and having unsatisfying social relationships. The greater degree of social stability of the control group is undoubtedly a factor in making their personalities more 'normal' or at least more stable.

It is regrettable that Douyon did not do a comparative study also testing rural peasant women who become possessed. They should, I think, show fewer of the 'abnormal' tendencies Douyon notes because they live in a more stable socio-cultural situation which provides ways to resolve the strains it creates. Their possessions, while full of individual psychological content, would be more the result of cultural molding than the expression of neurotic tendencies. If the urban women who become possessed are neurotic or psychotic it is because they have conflicts resulting from their early development and present life, for which no satisfying cultural pattern of resolution is provided. In their new setting the institution of possession, which they observed in their families during childhood, is both less culturally structured and less positively valued. Thus the new setting creates new problems for which it does not provide satisfactory means of resolution, and Douyon can classify the people who use the old forms in idiosyncratic rather than culturally constituted ways as abnormal.

No one has a neutral attitude toward possession. Everyone is for or against, even the women who become possessed. Many women in the experimental group were ambivalent. They liked being possessed because the Loa gave them information about themselves and others; events to come, traps to avoid, cures for family illnesses, and also the number for the national lottery, thus helping to lighten the burden of poverty on several levels at once. Possessions always have some goal. In transmitting the messages of the Loa the possessed person is actually trying to express through the Loa something he really wants known. Haitian peasants say, "vous vous cachez derrière un esprit pour mieux exprimer ce que vous voulez dire" (you hide behind a spirit to better express what you want to say — author's translation) (Douyon 1964: 234, 244, 254).

The women in Douyon's study who did not like being possessed resented their Loa because they 'compromised' them. They were embarrassed to have others know that they became possessed, preferring to be known as good Catholics, which would seem to indicate a desire for upward mobility and acceptance by the non-peasant milieu. Some Loa treat their devotees, male and female, badly, making them say and do things which they do not like, or making them so extravagant that they cause their families strife, or such is the traditional explanation for such behavior. Thus the subjects may have cause to be ashamed of the stupid things they say before strangers. In addition to the unpleasant memories, some people come out of possession with a residue of physical discomfort. Yet those women in the study who most disliked their Loa were not necessarily ready to get rid of them, nor had they made any attempt to do so. They would then be at the mercy of adversity with no protector. Some said they could not get rid of the Loa. If they joined Protestant churches to get away from Vodun they would then be possessed by the Holy Spirit. Some said they would soon begin to serve the Loa properly so that the Loa would stop mistreating them and making them behave so badly (Douyon 1964: 227, 233-236).

Such ambivalent and negative attitudes toward possession would seem to be the result of the urban setting in which these women are possessed. They would not be so embarrassed by their possessed behavior in the traditional setting because it would be normal, acceptable, and positively valued, whereas in the city it is seen as 'primitive', 'atavistic', and 'abnormal'. These women would obviously, from their attitudes, like to stray from their peasant roots and values, but they can not because they would have nothing to replace them and therefore would feel themselves totally lost.

Douyon states that possession would only be normal if it were limited to the acting out of ancestral gestures in a dramatic role play of the characters of mythological personages. However, behind the guise of the Loa is presented the internal drama of the individual personality. Many devotees are inhabited by well-known spirits, which they represent in their personal ways, and others are possessed by entities whose identity is surprising even to the devotees themselves (Douyon 1964: 232, 249). I do not agree that the individual's insertion of his own personality into the pattern of the deity personality is an indication of abnormality any more than it is for an actor to portray a certain character in a manner flavored by his own personality. And possession is much more than just dramatic role playing, because the devotees feel that they actually become their deities. Were these people as neurotic and psychotic as Douyon suggests, their ability to take on culturally stylized roles on cue, leaving them on cue also, and behaving in a manner recognizable to spectators as typical of a certain deity, would be surprising indeed. Of course in being possessed by a personally invented entity a person has a better chance of acting out personal neuroses, but again even this idiosyncratic acting out is performed within a culturally structured form.

Douyon considers that, due to the diversity of manifestations within the phenomenon of possession, it can not be reduced to a particular clinical entity. It "would seem that it is an original syndrome of the *backward country negroes' pathology* in so far as it is related to the *illiteracy—poverty—anxiety complex* of the Haitian socio-cultural context, and second to a disturbed, anxious, and depressed personality"[1]. Possession must be interpreted on the basis of the notion of despair, as an escape representing a symbolic death and rebirth to a new life (Douyon 1964: 8; 1965: 159).

Douyon is incorrect in seeing the possession syndrome as original and unique to Haiti, since it is found in similar form elsewhere in the New World and Africa, and because the origin of the Haitian

---

[1] Author's italics.

variety is found in West Africa. His term 'backward country negroes' pathology' sounds rather biased, and is not particularly accurate in respect to his particular research, since the women he studied lived in Port-au-Prince. Also, possession is the most supremely sacred act in a religious ritual, not merely a neurotic or psychotic manifestation as Douyon and other authors with more psychiatric than cultural points of view seem to totally forget or ignore. Therefore, it should be interpreted in a more positive light than just as a response to a miserable life situation. All of the people in the world who become possessed do not seem to be the victims of such dire circumstances, although such conditions undoubtedly do make a very positive contribution to having a propensity for possession. Possession represents a symbolic death and rebirth, but it represents death as a profane being and rebirth as a sacred one, namely a deity, which is an inherently positive act, as well as an escape from despair.

Douyon states that what is abnormal for an individual may not be abnormal for the society. Just because the behavior is frequently performed in rituals by some members of the group, it is not less fundamentally pathological in respect to the individual (1964: 8, 24). His implication is that such behavior is abnormal in terms of 'objective' criteria, meaning Western criteria, but that some societies institutionalize abnormal behavior. He is obviously not admitting that according to the culture and the society such behavior is normal, meaning, using Spiro's definition, that it is adaptive and provides for optimum functioning within the society, which it apparently does since people who become possessed are considered normal as opposed to the abnormal people who are victims of 'folie'.

Douyon states that even the authors who argue for the normality of possession must have recourse to the concept of pathology to explain certain forms of possession which in their unfolding conform less to archetypes or basic traditional models than to the dictates of the personal libido, which they do (e.g., Bastide 1950, 1960: passim). He states that people who stress its normality also fail to comment upon non-ritual as opposed to ritual possession. In such cases the factors of conditioning, learning, suggestion, role playing, the cathartic milieu, the hypnotic atmosphere, the hysteroform contagion, and the security of the group, apparently so active in ceremonies, do not exist (1964: 75). As is stated in the chapters on neurophysiology, hypnosis, and socialization, non-ceremonial possession need not be abnormal, and it is also a learned response to certain situations conforming to the belief system and world view of the community of Haitian peasants. Bastide and Mars admit that there are pathological cases of possession, but that they are very exceptional (Bastide 1953: 14; Mars 1946: 95).

According to Landes, doctors from a local insane asylum were struck by how few members of the Bahian Candomblé became insane. The emotional and social outlets provided by the religious group were apparently unusually satisfying (1947: 78). Bastide reports that members of the traditional Afro-Brazilian cults are specimens of good mental and physical health. These cults are factors in producing psychophysical equilibrium in emphasizing the control of the individual unconscious by cultural patterns with great religious significance (1950: 251).

Douyon does consider possession to be a positive mechanism in preventing more serious mental illness. He states that the psychological equilibrium of the possessed individuals is preserved thanks to the homeostatic function of possession, which involves, along with a very infantile reaction of the personality, institutionalized regression in the service of adaptation. It also represents a process of primitive psychoanalysis in which material comes out of the depths of the personality which can not be expressed in any other way (1965: 8, 256; 1967: 5).

De Heusch, commenting on the Songhay possession cult, says that the technique of the zima (priest) radically reverses the fundamental concepts of psychoanalysis because instead of trying to exorcise the evil or demon it accepts the evil or sickness and canalizes it to new, acceptable and valued ends. It is efficacious because a state which may have become permanent or uncontrollably intermittent now only comes when ordered. A human order is imposed on the manifestations of the deities (1962: 137). Thus if the individual really is neurotic or psychotic, his religion helps him to gain sufficient control over his malady to manifest it in a certain form, on certain cues, for a specified period of time. Those people who do not fit their manifestations into the designated framework are considered insane.

The religious community furnishes members of the society with a certain number of well-known consecrated modes of divinity personalities characteristic of certain libidinous attitudes within which individual conflicts may contain and express themselves rather than to flare into neurotic symptoms (Bastide 1950: 256). All kinds of tendencies may be fitted into the varied deity personalities. A religious style is imposed upon disturbed psychic manifestations and order is created out of psychic chaos. The sick or potentially sick person is given a behavioral language in which to express himself. Possession is the language of the gods (de Heusch 1962: 138; 1965: 149-150). Instead of having one's problems solved on the level of everyday profane society, those of the possessed are removed to the sacred plane of the mythical society of the gods whose gestures they act out (Duvignand 1959: 257).

Douyon notes that in Haiti, phenomena such as suicide, homosexuality, alcoholism, and delinquency are relatively absent or reflect more an understandable reaction to a life situation than profound emotional pathology. There is undoubtedly an intimate relationship between possession, depression states, and suicide. The annual rate of crime until recent years has been paradoxically low in comparison with the high population density, stress of poverty, and constant frustration of so many basic needs. Recourse to the Vodun deities is a constant source of stimulation and comfort. Much animosity and aggression must be built up in such a climate, and possession is, according to Douyon, the only alternative to venting such feelings on one's self or others. In the psychodrama of possession these emotions can be acted out. Possession keeps people from committing suicide because they can step out of their miserable lives from time to time. The inhibitory effect of possession on homicide and suicide in Haiti and elsewhere should be checked empirically and statistically correlated (Douyon 1964: 255; 1967: 1, 6).

I would maintain that the evidence that people who get possessed are abnormal is not at all conclusive given the relativity of culturally determined reality. Also the chapters on neurophysiology and hypnosis indicate, as Douyon agrees, that similar states can be produced by neurophysiological stimuli and/or hypnosis in perfectly normal individuals who are not of a milieu where possession exists. The argument for abnormality is too open to criticism on various levels to be acceptable. Some people who get possessed are apparently abnormal, and would undoubtedly be more so if they did not get possessed, but the evidence would seem to indicate that the majority of people who become possessed are quite normal. Possession appears to be a functional institution for good mental health.

It would be interesting to observe what the relationship is between possession and forms of deviant behavior found in the societies in question. What kinds of people are classified as deviant in terms of folk theory? Are they only those who are considered insane in the sense described in the chapter on mental illness or are there others, and if so what are they like behaviorally and psychodynamically? Do they get possessed or not, and if so is their possession normal or abnormal? Belo reports that a man considered deviant from the norm in a particular Balinese village maintained a similar difference while entranced (1960). Are there people who in Western terms would be hysterics or neurotics who do not become possessed (I would imagine the psychotics would be those people considered insane), and if not, how do they manifest their problems? Douyon suggests that it would be useful to do a comparative survey of personality patterns with Rorschach tests on members of various populations who are subject to ritual seizures, such as in Togo, Dahomey, Haiti, and Brazil, to see if the typology of trance and possession states correlates with similar or different personality structures (1967: 7). Such a study should also consider possible rural-urban, traditional-acculturated variables, and take greater account of specific cultural factors than was done in Douyon's personality study.

CONCLUSION

Our normal waking consciousness ... is but one special type of consciousness, whilst all about it, parted from it by the filmiest of screens, there lie potential forms of consciousness entirely different. We may go through life without suspecting their existence; but apply the requisite stimulus, and at a touch they are there in all their completeness, definite types of mentality which probably somewhere have their field of application and adaptation. No account of the universe in its totality can be final which leaves these other forms of consciousness quite disregarded. How to regard them is the question — for they are so discontinuous with ordinary consciousness, yet they may determine attitudes though they cannot furnish formulas, and open a region though they fail to give a map. At any rate they forbid a premature closing of our accounts with reality (William James 1902: 378-379).

Each society selects a certain range and spectrum of human behavioral possibilities to elaborate and institutionalize, leaving unelaborated and outside of the spectrum many experiential possibilities. Some societies elaborate a very broad range of human possibilities, others do not, and what is normal in one may be considered abnormal in another. Within their spectra some societies include trance and possession phenomena, states seen in most of Western society as characteristic of unstable personalities because they indicate a lack of self-control. These societies exploit the capacity of some individuals to experience such states for the good of the society, in institutionalizing them as the means par excellence of communicating with the supernatural beings who control man's life. In being possessed by deities and spirits members of the community are allowed to deal directly with these all-important beings. Thus they, because of their own behavioral propensities, can have experiences beyond the normal conscious limits of most people, and can allow others to feel such experiences vicariously, in addition to providing the link between the gods and man.

Haitian poets inspired by Vodun possession see in it a way to go beyond the normal limits of human experience to know another, very meaningful and very different kind of reality. "... les poètes voient en lui le moyen d'atteindre l'absolu par les dérèglements des sens. La raison lucide mise en veilleuse, l'instinct reprend ses droits et, grâce aux trances extatiques, permet de parvenir à une réalité plus fondamentale" (... poets see in it the way to attain the absolute by the deranging of the senses. With lucid reason dimmed, instinct recovers its rights and, thanks to the ecstatic trances, allows one to arrive at a more fundamental reality — author's translation) (Hoffman 1960-61: 203). This is actually what possession is as a religious ritual. The participants exist on a sacred, more meaningful plane, having left their profane beings in order to become gods. What is experienced in the possession state is not unreal because it is not within the normal realm of logical, conscious life, but more real because it is interpreted as a divine experience.

It has been stressed throughout this study that possession is a complex phenomenon provoked by a concatenation of diverse factors working together in different combinations. The specific factors involved and their relative importance determine the nature of the possession experience, along with social, cultural, and psychological factors which influence which of the causative elements are involved, and to what degree. The factor or factors of predominant importance vary from society to society and situation to situation.

The most fundamental element in possession is the presence of neurophysiological changes from the normal waking state which result in this particular altered state of consciousness. Such neurophysiological changes are most frequently produced by sensory bombardment, usually in the form of the sonic driving of the drum rhythms. The effects of the drums are heightened by the simultaneous rhythmic stimulation of other sensory receptors because the participants are dancing, singing, and moving together in close proximity in a ceremonial atmosphere in which possession manifesting the presence of the gods is expected. These neurophysiological effects may be reinforced by somatic factors such as fatigue, hypoglycemia from fasting, and hyperventilation from the rhythmic, energetic dancing.[1] The effects of the sonic driving alone suffice to produce hallucinations and other sensory distortions and feelings of strangeness, which are amplified and given content and meaning by the other elements involved in ceremonial possession. Non-ceremonial possession is a result of the body's neuro-

[1] A professor of mine noted feeling strange at times while attending Pentecostal church services. In thinking over the factors involved he realized that the rhythm of the music and voices was causing him to breathe heavily and rhythmically in time with it, giving him a slight case of hyperventilation, which caused the strange feelings.

physiological and psychological response to situations of extreme stress.[1] It is difficult, sometimes impossible, to separate the purely neurophysiological elements in possession from the other elements, as illustrated in the chapter on cultural determinism. However, sometimes people seem to be reacting just to the effects of the drums. An example of this would be the Haitians who become 'saoulé' (drunk) by the gods. They show an initial response to the rhythmic stimulation, but consciously fight against the new sensations rather than reinforcing them with cultural and psychological material. Also, Douyon notes that Haitian men involved in Vodun, rather than going into an actual trance, show its psycho-motor equivalent which calmly ends before the real, dramatic, rowdy possessions of the women begin (1964: 47). The induction period and the early uncontrolled possessions, before the deity is baptized, may be largely neurophysiological effects, although there is also personal, as opposed to culturally determined, psychological content. Some people have more of a propensity for neurophysiological variations than others, and this propensity seems to be hereditary, as possession usually is.

The element of hypnosis also plays an important role in possession. The hypnotic state is triggered by the altered state of consciousness and change in body ego produced by the neurophysiological effects of the rhythmic drumming. The transference relationship has as objects the priest, who persuasively and authoritatively directs the devotees, the deities who are responsible for and in control of all the possessed devotees' behavior, and the community of spectators who support and protect the possessed participants. The actual hypnotist is really the subject himself, who, given certain stimuli, recalls and re-enacts more or less automatically a style of behavior impressed upon him during an initiation period and/or which he has observed closely while growing up. The stimuli provoke the expression of the new conditioned responses inculcated in the lethargic state of the initiation period. The content of this auto-hypnotic behavior is highly motivated for both socio-cultural and psychological reasons, and is the culturally defined personality of a deity. Non-ceremonial possession may be likened to spontaneous hypnotic states in response to great stress or anxiety. The god personality is the manifestation of a subsystem

---

[1] Also, experienced priests and priestesses may deliberately invoke their deities on non-ceremonial occasions for consultation or other reasons.

within the ego, developed and given a specific form chosen from the varied possibilities available in the culture. There are social and psychological features which make populations and individuals differentially susceptible to hypnotoform states such as possession.

Individual psychology plays an important role in possession because it is a state in which the normal psychological, as well as social, restrictions and definitions do not hold. In this state the devotee can express facets of himself which are normally not expressed or which are just not consciously developed, plus fulfill wishes and compensate for shameful or forbidden desires and impulses. This factor makes the attainment of such a state and the behavior manifest therein highly desirable to the devotee, consciously and unconsciously. Because of various psychological and social needs some people are more susceptible than others to hypnotoform states, and particularly to possession as a special version of such states. It is necessary to have a positive psychological impetus to reinforce the neurophysiological effects of the drumming and to permit the hypnotic state to develop.

Possession in the societies in question is usually a positively valued social phenomenon observed on many social occasions, and part of the learned behavior of the socialization process. In a world peopled by various non-human as well as human beings, children are taught that the former have an existence as real as the latter, although different. These non-human beings may be seen, or in some way perceived, in the events of ordinary life, and some may take over the control of the bodies and minds of the people. Hence in this type of environment the individual grows up expecting to have intimate relationships with such beings, to the point of having his total being taken over by one on certain types of occasions on which such an occurrence is expected and culturally approved. When such a take-over is by a deity or spirit it may be the supreme act in a religious ceremony, or the deity's coming to the person's aid in a moment of need. When the possessing agent is an angry or evil deity or spirit the effect will be sickness, ill fortune, or insanity. Even the manifestations of benevolent possessing agents must be socialized or they can get out of hand leading to insanity. Socialized ceremonial possession, being of benefit to the whole community, is a positive phenomenon resulting in attention, respect, and admiration for the individuals involved. They serve their own personal interests, and vicariously those of the spectators, plus strengthening social solidarity through this collective religious experience.

It is, of course, the cultural beliefs which make the phenomenon of possession an approved and valuable institution, structure and define it and give it content, and provide a role and function for it in the life of the community. The world view is of a universe in which man can enter into close relationships with supernatural beings who may come into the individual's body and assume total responsibility for it, accounting for changes in individual behavior and personal fate, as well as explaining the nature of the universe and of man. Thus it is ultimately the belief system and values of the society which determine the existence, nature, and psycho-social function of the complex altered state of consciousness known in folk theory as possession. It is the cultural beliefs which make possession a positive phenomenon in the societies in question, a psychological propensity for which, inculcated by the socialization process, reinforces and lends positive impetus to the basic neurophysiological and hypnotic infrastructure of the state. They provide the deity personalities which mold the behavioral responses to the neurophysiological and psychological changes basic to such states but manifest in different ways in different socio-cultural settings.

Within a particular culture and cross-culturally possession behavior may take various forms.[1] It may first be ceremonial or non-ceremonial. It may take place in a specifically ritual setting where it is the supreme act of religious expression for the devotees, or spontaneously with no ceremonial reference. Ceremonial possession may be controlled or uncontrolled. The possessions of normal experienced people are controlled and thus approved. Initial possessions, before the individual becomes habituated to and learns

---

[1] According to de Heusch the various possible forms of possession institutions can be classified as follows (1965: 154):
- possession as illness—the irruption in the self of a maleficent personality foreign to the self.
- mixture—possession is initially seen as an illness. It is cured by being transformed into sacred theater—such as in the Zar cult.
- Vodun—an extension of the theatrical beyond the therapeutic treatment which it sometimes completes. Possession is deliberately sought for its beneficial effects and comforts. Initiation provides the path to physical, psychic, and metaphysical health.

De Heusch is also taking into consideration in his first type possession in societies with no institution of collective ceremonial possession, but where people may be possessed when they are upset or because they are or are to be diviners or mediums. His typology does not include individualistic possession in societies with institutional possession, and there is often not such a clear distinction between his second and third types within indigenous theory.

to control his deity, are uncontrolled, the aim of initiation being to impose a cultural form on these chaotic manifestations and teach the devotee to control his possessions. The possession-like behavior of people culturally defined as insane tends to be by definition uncontrolled and uncontrollable, for if not, the individual would be considered normal. Also uncontrolled and violent are the possessions of people who are being punished by their deities for some misdeed. According to Bowers, the Haitians realize that the mass possession state could get out of hand if not carefully controlled by the priest and drummers. The increasing frenzy, if uncontrolled, could easily lead to acts of violence (1961: 279).

In addition to these differences in behavioral manifestations, possessions may vary in degree of involvement, which is related to the number, combination, and intensity of the factors involved. Possession may go from the most superficial level, in which one may wonder if the devotee is sincere, to the most profound level, when the individual is so totally carried away that he becomes unconscious, loses all control, and must be carried out in the midst of a psychological storm bordering on pathology. Cultural control may be present, in various degrees, from the pole of virtual total cultural control to the opposite pole of a total lack of cultural structuring in nearly or purely pathological manifestations. Huxley reports the existence in Haiti of what is known as a "prise des yeux" (seizure of the eyes), in which a person is possessed without losing consciousness of himself. He can see himself while his body is carried through various motions by the possessing Loa (1966: 210). Such is probably the state of the houngans who officiate quite efficiently while possessed.

It is evident from the text that in the types of societies being considered, those with the cultural institution of collective ceremonial possession of devotees by supernatural beings, there are various forms of possession which are provoked by different combinations of factors, and which have different cultural, social, and psychological significance. The basis of the various possessions in normal individuals is neurophysiological and hypnotic or auto-hypnotic. These two factors work together, elements of each being somewhat involved in the other. These factors, then, provide the common base, which may be elaborated in various kinds of ways. The varieties of elaborations of the basic state may be seen as a continuum from pure drama almost to its polar opposite, the expression of personal, idiosyncratic impulses, the difference being the degree of influence of the cultural environment relative to the degree of individual psychological input.

I would broadly classify the types of possession manifestations within the societies in question (and generalize to other societies with analogous institutions) as:

1. Predominantly cultural.
2. Cultural and psychological in relatively equal proportions.
3. Predominantly psychological.

Type one, predominantly cultural possession, is actually highly motivated, theatrical role playing, as exemplified by the traditional Dahomean possession cults. In the Dahomean cults people were chosen as devotees of a particular deity whom they served exclusively, and only in specific, very structured circumstances. People were typically chosen for the priesthood in one of three ways: they were promised at birth to the deity who had allowed their mothers to conceive after a long wait; they could be chosen by other members of their family to incarnate a family deity; or if a member of the family was ill or suffering ill fortune, some member of the family, not necessarily or even usually the victim, was chosen to serve a deity who would help the afflicted person.

People chosen in such diverse ways, and most likely sharing no other common traits beyond a similar socialization experience, would have to learn to undergo the ritual depersonalization and dissociation of actual possession. This is all the more true because the deities were not chosen to conform to the personalities of the devotees, allowing them to express unexpressed facets of themselves. Herskovits notes that the regimentation of cult life weakened the intensity of the trance in comparison with more spontaneous possession observable elsewhere. In Dahomey the dancers seemed rarely, if ever, to be completely entranced, even at the point of greatest frenzy, and informers noted that the greatest gratification gotten by the devotees was the pleasure of dressing up, playing the role of an exalted being, and receiving the attention and admiration of the spectators (1938: 180, 199). There was, however, little gratification of specific unfulfilled wishes except for the desire to exhibit oneself and be the center of attention.

Bastide notes that in the traditional Candomblé people often act out roles which only correspond to a social imposition and are not specifically related to their own personalities (1950: 257). Here, as in Dahomey, people may become devotees because they were born when a certain god cured their mothers' infertility, or as a result of being cured by a god of an illness.

It is not clear to what extent these examples of what I term cultural possession occur in the other traditional West African society in question, the Songhay Holey cult. Except for the cases of faking I would not expect to find much cultural possession in the Zar cult because of its role as a healing institution which people join to rechannel their disturbed tendencies. This type of possession may exist to some extent in the most traditional parts of rural Haiti, but probably not to a very great degree, and it is apparently not prevalent in the Brazilian cults other than the traditional Yoruba Candomblé.

The manner in which people selected for such diverse reasons all learn to assume the role of their deities in the more or less dissociated state of possession is through the new conditioning of the initiation period. In traditional Dahomey where there was least rapport between the individual's personality and that of his deity the initiation period was normally about seven years, which the individual spent in seclusion learning to become his deity. In the Candomblé also, initiation is important though considerably briefer, usually a few months. During this time a totally new secondary personality is imposed on the novice with a whole set of newly conditioned responses to the ceremonial stimuli to be triggered on cue in the proper atmosphere. The importance of the initiation period declines as the type of possession tends toward the psychological end of the continuum since the culturally patterned roles to be learned become less structured and may cease to exist.

The neurophysiological and hypnotic factors given content by the religious system are particularly important in this cultural possession because the specific psychological motivation is absent. Because the psychological element is lacking and because of the rigid structure, cultural possession is probably considerably less therapeutic than the varieties approaching the other end of the spectrum.

In the second type of possession there is deliberate rapport between the deity personality and that of the individual who is chosen to serve him. Care is taken to insure the proper matching of deity and devotee, since trouble will result if the choice is incorrect. The individual may exhibit facets of his personality normally hidden from himself and others, in the guise of the deity, thus in culturally approved form. This is apparently recognized and freely admitted by members of the society, judging by the Haitian and Dahomean statements previously quoted. Some initiation is often necessary to teach the individual to mold his usually initially disorganized self-expression to the cultural mold provided. Neurophysiological changes and hypnotic factors are also important in this type, but relatively less so than in type one because of the great psychological impetus. The individual is highly motivated to play a role in which he can acceptably express, with group approval, tendencies and attitudes which he must normally repress.

It is reasonable to assume that the deity personalities provided by a specific society would correspond to the particular kinds of personality structures, cultural ideals and values, features of social differentiation, and conflicts and tensions engendered by the socio-cultural system. This type of possession is probably usually deeper, and both more gratifying and more therapeutic than type one. It is more beneficial to individuals and to the community because it allows both cultural values and social structural elements, which might otherwise cause covert strains and conflicts, to be expressed on a supernatural plane on which the members of the society can deal with and sometimes resolve them, at least symbolically. On this more meaningful plane they are expressed, understood, and dealt with, the effects of which are very beneficial to the ordinary day-to-day functioning of the society. This second type of possession is the most common and is characteristic of all of the African and Afro-American groups in question with the exception of traditional Dahomey.

The third type of possession is typically found in situations where the possession cult is in a state of disorganization, usually because it is no longer the religion of a coherent, well-integrated community. In such a situation, where cultural determinism and control are lacking, possessions tend to be expressions of the individual's own private impulses, with no cultural mold, hence their content is idiosyncratic rather than culturally determined, and may tend toward pathology. This type of possession is particularly found in the non-traditional groups in Haiti and Brazil. One of its major defining characteristics is the individual invention of private possessing agents corresponding to the impulses striving for expression. It follows that this type of possession may quite easily tend toward or be symptomatic of neurosis since it is not culturally controlled, but is rather the use of the form of a cultural institution for the individual's private purposes.

Initiation does not exist for this type of possession although people regularly initiated to be the devotees of traditional deities may also have such personal deities, usually in this case dead relatives or close friends. Neurophysiological and hypnotic changes are less important in this type of possession than any of the others because the provocation is almost purely psychological.

The extreme of purely psychological possession is found in insane people who have religious delusions involving persecution by traditional deities. Their insanity is evidenced by the fact that although their world views are similar to those of the normal members of the society, they can not use the cultural molds to deal with the world they perceive, but do so in a way which is totally idiosyncratic in terms of the social norms of their society.

Each type of possession is characterized by a specific kind of possessing agent, the character of which is directly related to the nature of the possession and its role in the society. These possessing agents vary in: importance in the universe, human attributes, proximity to and intimacy of their relationship with man, and the degree of the individual's involvement and self-expression in the possession.

In type one possession the possessing agents are powerful nature deities concerned with the functioning of the universe and the life of the whole community. The Nigerian and Bahian Orisha, Dahomean Vodun, and to some degree the Songhay Holey and original Haitian Loa are deities of this type. Such deities are part of a coherent, complex mythological structure, and the possession ritual actually consists in the re-enacting of the lives of the gods or deified ancestors, as in the cases of traditional Nigeria, Dahomey, and Bahia. These deities are very far from man and embody very universal and general human attributes. These deities do not live in a very intimate relationship with man and do not interfere with his day-to-day life. In Haiti, the Loa of relatively recent vintage live in natural features of the environment and are intimately involved in the lives of their devotees, to the point even of marrying them. The Bahian Orisha, on the contrary, must come from Africa to possess their devotees, and are therefore less accessible. In Nigeria and Dahomey the individual is not really deeply involved in his possession, both because he is not actually expressing his own personality but merely playing an important role, and also because of the stature and awesomeness of the beings to be represented.

In the second type of possession the entities involved are rather minor deities, spirits, or human personages. The Loa and Holey are gods or spirits, close to and intimately involved with man, although concerned with the workings of the universe. Such beings are actually more concerned with the intricacies of human life than with more cosmic issues. The Zar are essentially spirits, apparently not in control of nature, who are concerned with man's everyday behavior and who intervene whenever necessary. In Haiti many Loa have been invented which reflect purely Haitian social realities, many representing typical Haitian human categories, although their characters are made to conform to what is seen as ideal rather than what is really the case. The Songhay Haouka are personages from the European society which had begun to impinge upon the Songhay when the Haouka came into being. Perhaps by being possessed by such personages the Songhay felt that they were coping with this new influence and absorbing some of its power.

It is essential for the devotee's personality to coincide with that of the deity or spirit possessing him, which is quite reasonable since the characteristics, attitudes, and appetites of the possessing beings are very human, though they are more powerful, aggressive, and domineering. The deity may come to the individual in a dream or by possessing him in a ceremony, or the individual may show symptoms indicating that a deity wants him as a devotee. The identity of the deity is determined by a diviner and the person is initiated and taught to serve his new master.

There is great leeway for self-expression in the guise of these deities and spirits because each person is expected to portray his deity in a manner corresponding to his own character. In the cultural possession ceremonies the emphasis is on the re-enactment of mythology, and the mythology is considered important in everyday life to the point that the mythological relationships and behavior of the deities are actually believed to determine the lives of their devotees. On the contrary, in ceremonies of possession of the second type ritual is more important than mythology, the latter sometimes being almost non-existent as in Haiti and in the Shango cult of Trinidad. Acts attributed to the supernatural beings are integrated into secular history and secular heroes are placed in the religious pantheon, like Toussaint and Dessalines in Haiti, revolutionary heroes who are now Loa in the Vodun pantheon. People become possessed by these heroes and act out their characters and attitudes in ceremonies. The devotees are concerned more with the likes and dislikes of the deities, and their activities and personalities, than with any explanatory theology. The personalities of the deities may change over time quite easily since there is no formal mythology and the dynamic informal mythology will incorporate the deities' supposed involvement in human life which effected these personality changes. The rituals in which the personalities and activities of the deities are acted out, are 'ethnodramas' dealing with the realities of daily social life. In this type of possession one could say that the human social interaction determines the interaction of the deities when they come to the ceremonies. The possessed individuals, rather than re-enacting the lives and acts of the deities, are actually re-enacting on a sacred level their ordinary profane social interactions and tensions.

In the third type of possession the possessing agents are not cultural deities or spirits, but rather personifications of individual libidinous attitudes, or actual people known by the possessed individual. These beings initially come to the individual to introduce themselves on different types of occasions, frequently during sleep. No initiation is possible since the possessing being is not part of an established institution. The possession consists of the acting out of the individual's own impulses in a very personal ritual with little or no structured cultural influence. If there is cultural control it seems to be limited to provoking and terminating, but not internally structuring the possession experience, like the use of holy water to end Catimbó possession. As cultural control decreases, the possibility of abnormality increases because what is normal is what is culturally expected, and since the content of this third type of possession is only minimally controlled by the culture, some of its manifestations may fall outside of cultural expectations.

These three types of deities and possessions reflect different aspects of reality. The deities of the first type, being concerned with the natural elements and their control, reflect the structure and workings of the universe, and man's relationship to it. Since these deities control the universe it is reasonable that their behavior should determine that of their devotees. Deities of the second type reflect the structure and values of the society. New deities and spirits are developed in conformity to new needs within the society, exemplified by the creole deities in Haiti and the Haouka among the Songhay. Possessing agents of the third type reflect the inner psychic drama of the individuals involved, and the content of such possessions should reveal what kinds of tensions and conflicts are typically engendered in its members by the society.

Huxley notes that in Haiti there are three categories of forces characterized by the Loa, which shape the society. The Rada are the original Loa who are from the Dahomean city of Allada (from whence the name), plus other 'nations' of Loa such as the Congo, Angola or Wangol, and the Ibo (1966: 205). These Loa tend to be like the type one great nature deities in their concerns although they may not be any different in their relationship to men than the Loa of less ultimate concerns.

The Petro Loa are often the gods of other 'nations' or are the wrathful aspects of the Rada Loa. Ogun is Ogun Jé-Rouge (red eyes), and this suffix is added to characterize Agové, Erzulie, Damballah, and others. They are patrons of rage, sudden disastrous whims, even sorcery, in which they can exorcise as well as bedevil. They are much concerned with healing (Huxley 1966: 205). These Petro Loa were developed from the Haitian experience of slavery, revolution, and a stratified society in which the peasants, principle practitioners of the Vodun religion, live in misery. There is no clear dichotomy between Rada and Petro Loa except in temperament. It would be a bit forced to make a rigid classification of the Rada as type one and the Petro Loa as type two within my framework for analysing possession phenomena. The distinctions exist as far as their domains of interest are concerned, but not in their actual behavior and relationship to man.

The third category of Loa shaping Haitian society would be the numerous new Loa with no definite place in the traditional pantheon. The old deities are not sufficient to give form to the new problems. This third category, which does correlate with my type three, consists of the possessing agents created by the individuals out of their own particular troubles. They sometimes achieve patronage of a houmfort (cult center), but they are usually just the working Loa of small oracular shrines which have a clientele but no real congregation (Huxley 1966: 205).

Both the form and the content of possession phenomena mirror the degree of coherence and integration of the social and cultural milieu. In the traditional cults social norms and cultural values triumph over individual impulses, whereas in the non-traditional, less cohesive situations, individual impulses reign. According to Bastide, when group control diminishes, mysticism changes from the expression of collective models to the individual expressions of the experiences people are undergoing as a result of social change (1960: 524-526). The traditional socio-cultural system provides a setting in which even personalities which in Western society would be considered unstable because of their propensity for dissociation are accepted and may play a valued role as long as they adhere to the dictates of the society. With the dissolution of the structure which provides such direction, people with these propensities are left to their own devices, and their possession manifestations become more individualistic and more potentially pathological.

Possession itself is thus neither all normal nor all abnormal, but may be either for different individuals, and perhaps even for the same individual under different circumstances. It is important to examine the role of and attitude toward possession in specific societies to know which it is under what circumstances. In the societies in question possession is not in general considered abnormal, but is rather a sign of election by the gods. The mechanisms involved, which consist of what in Western terms would be considered pathological dissociation, are unacceptable in these societies only if they fail to conform to the culturally predetermined framework. The social group requires that such behavior occur only under certain conditions and that it be considered the work of the gods, not of man. Where group support fails or when the manifestation does not follow the cultural dictates, it becomes pathological in the eyes of the society.[1]

It is not possible to say that all possession is either normal or abnormal because this depends upon its meaning and form within a given socio-cultural context. If it is strictly controlled, culturally stylized ceremonial behavior it is most apt to be a normal hypnotoform phenomenon, hypnosis being more easily provoked in

---

[1] Louis Mars distinguishes three types of possession in Haiti (in Bowers 1961: 270):
1. that which occurs during religious ritual in which the behavior conforms to the expected cultural patterns.
2. possession during ceremonies that does not conform to the cultural stereotypes.
3. possession which occurs spontaneously outside of ritual occasions. This type may be the most pathological.
Kiev says that possession in Haiti may be (1961b: 136):
    — applauded in some circumstances — mainly ceremonies.
    — vaguely tolerated in others — spontaneous possession in social situations, like the market.
    — frowned upon or condemned in other contexts and when differing in degree of control — folie.

normal people, than in neurotics or psychotics. Where this cultural
control is lacking, possession is likely to approach hysteria. In the
societies that do not have culturally determined ceremonial
possession, and where people become possessed when upset or in
situations of tension, the 'possession' may actually be a case of
hysteria. Possession approaches hysteria as cultural control over the
expressions of the individuals' personal impulses diminishes. It is
important to know the purpose of the possession cult and its role
within the society to understand the phenomenon. The Zar cult is
considered a healing cult for disturbed people, whereas the other
possession cults in question are actually religious institutions for the
worship of the gods of the community. Hence the Zar cult would
probably include more people considered abnormal by their own
society and by the outside observer than would the other cults, into
which people are initiated to learn to serve their deities, not because
they are ill, although illness is sometimes a symptom that a deity
wants the individual as a devotee.

The non-traditional versions of all of the cults in question probably
have more abnormal people than the traditional versions because of
the decrease of cultural control and support. The disturbances which
cause people to join a healing cult may be anything from frustrated
status ambitions to actual mental illness. Those possession cults
designed for religious worship rather than healing are frequently
therapeutic although this is not their primary intent. Most religious
systems have therapeutic functions in that they give a sense of well-
being and provide a way of understanding, reacting to, and coping
with all the aspects and vicissitudes of life. Despite such therapeutic
value, religions, including those in which the supreme manifestation
is spirit possession, can not be looked upon merely as psychiatric
clinics.

Given the various factors involved in the different types of
possession, it does not seem that any simple correlation can be found
between personality characteristics and susceptibility to possession.
The socialization process in a society where possession is a valued
institution may create a general propensity for trance states in most
members of the society. Some people, however, probably undergo
neurophysiological changes and the resulting altered state of
consciousness with greater ease than others. Also some are probably
in structural positions which might tend to make them particularly
susceptible to possession, as is the case with women in most societies.

The chapter on socialization indicated that radically different child-rearing practices in societies with totally different cultural systems may produce similar type behavior, though it will differ in form, content, role, and meaning in the total society. It is possible that similar personality traits would perhaps be found in the same category of possession, as I have established them, but empirical proof would be needed to substantiate such a hypothesis, and numerous social and cultural variables would have to be taken into account.

It must be emphasized that the degree of normality or abnormality of possession is not important per se. These elements are important in determining the role, function, and meaning of possession in the total socio-cultural scheme, and for the individuals involved. Bourguignon notes that Brazilian anthropologist and psychiatrist René Ribeiro studied individual Candomblé members who became possessed and found that the significance of the experience varied from individual to individual. A blanket statement that characterizes possession as normal, pathological, prophylactic, etc., does not come to grips with the reality of the situation. What superficially appears to be the same phenomenon implies different things to different people (1965: 44). Hence the function of possession in the realm of the mental health of the members of the society must be considered in relation to the role of the institution of possession in the total society, since the latter determines the former.

According to Julian Huxley, character consists of a number of attitudes summed up physically in a man's posture, the total way he carries himself, and neurosis or nervousness is another name for an accumulation of tension in the musculature. These tensions are half-acted attitudes which a man stores in himself. These attitudes are, Huxley stresses, bodily attitudes (1966: 208). Such half-acted attitudes may be expressed in societies without possession as emanations from the unconscious during dreams, but then they are purely mental mechanisms. The dreamer passively witnesses the unrolling of his psychological state like a spectator in a movie. In possession, however, he identifies his total being with various elements of his psychological make-up and this mental mechanism is translated into action. The individual acts out bodily these elements of his personality in terms of the behavior patterns of the deities of his religious system (Mars 1951: 649-650). It would appear that such a total, as opposed to a purely passive and mental, expression of these half-developed elements of the personality, in a situation of ceremonial social interaction, would be a very satisfying release for the tensions built up from their previous lack of expression. They can be actively expressed in possession as opposed to their passive expression in dreaming, because their active manifestation is subject to definite socio-cultural control and patterning.

It follows within Huxley's theory that the various and perhaps contradictory attitudes which a man has acquired in the process of growing up and coping with life possess him as Loa (or Orisha, Zar, Winti, etc.). They are then seen as having a separate existence from himself because during possession his body is a mere physical receptacle for the deity's personality which has displaced one of his own souls. Instead of being obedient to external figures who possess his will, however, the devotee actually becomes obedient to a part of himself (1966: 217). "More precisely he has reintrojected previously projected feelings, attitudes, impulses, and drives" (Wittkower 1964: 76). This part of himself to which he is obedient is a facet only partially developed by previous experience but not usually overtly expressed. On certain occasions, ritual or stressful, this facet, more appropriate to the situation, takes possession of him.

This reintrojection of previously projected attitudes is very similar to Leinhardt's interpretation of the relationship between Powers and Divinity and human experience in Dinka religion in the Sudan. The Powers are supernatural entities which represent images of the Dinkas' reactions to and interpretations of their experiences in their physical and social environment. They see these images not as memories of the past existing only in their minds and influencing them from this angle, as would be the case in the Western world, but rather as part of objective reality, which can act upon them at any time as outside agents. Dinka encounters with ghosts, an imaging of one kind of experience, take place only in encounters with oneself, as in dreams. The human being acted upon by the Power is seen as passive, as in the horse and rider analogy common to all of the possession cults being considered, in which the devotee is likened to a horse and the possessing deity to the rider. The Powers which compose Divinity image man's manifold experience in the world. The Powers are distinct as man's experiences are distinct, but united in Divinity as man's diverse experiences are united in the self (1961: 147-157). Thus the Dinka see past experiences as continuing to act upon and influence them as active agents with themselves as passive receptors. They do not contemplate events, but feel that they have a perpetual, independent existence which forces men to continue to experience them with their total beings. "Their world is not for them an object of study, but an active subject . . ." (Leinhardt 1961: 156).

The Loa and the other deities and spirits in these possession cults are like the Dinka Powers. They represent images of both group and individual, common and significant human experiences that are projected into the supernatural sphere and then seen to act on people by taking possession of their bodies and minds. The deities which possess people are elements of themselves, developed or partially developed from past experience, which come to the fore on certain occasions and become the ruling force in the devotees' existence for a moment.

The deities, like the Powers, since they reflect human experience, will reflect the social structure and interaction of the group, imaging social experience and attitudes toward it in symbolic form. The personalities and interaction of the deities reflect not only social roles, but also the attitudes of the community toward them. Leinhardt reports that among the Dinka there has been a general rise in the number of free-divinities not linked to traditional social structural elements, but potentially equally affecting all Dinkas as individuals and families. These free-divinities correspond to the recognition of increasing individualism in Dinka life, and are intimations of changes in the basic structure of the society. New experiences such as that of influence from outside of the society have been assimilated to the experience imaged in free-divinities. It is possible that they are seen as 'seizing' men more powerfully as powerful external influences have impinged upon the Dinka (1961: 163-169).

These free-divinities may be likened to the possessing beings in the third and to some degree the second type of possession. They have arisen to image and provide a way to cope with new types of experience not prefigured in the traditional scheme. They also reflect the growth of individualism with the breakdown of the traditional structure. The creole deities in Haiti, who are peasants, mulattoes, and revolutionary heroes, and the Songhay Haouka, who are kings, secretaries, generals, etc., evidently reflect a reality different from that of traditional times. The Haitian deities represent the history of the country, and the Songhay deities, the encroachment of Western civilization. Both the Haitian creole Petro deities and the Haouka are of more violent character and possess their devotees more vigorously

than the traditional deities, reflecting the violence and conflict of
Haitian history and the conflict and shock of the Western
impingement on the Songhay.

In imaging their reactions to experience in physical and social
reality, and separating the active subject from the passive object in
experience, the Dinka and the societies with possession cults have
"... the possibility of creating a form of experience they desire, and
of freeing themselves symbolically from what they must otherwise
passively endure" (Leinhardt 1961: 170). In projecting their reactions
to experience onto a symbolic supernatural level they reify them and
give them some generally known and accepted emotional value. On
this sacred level they can manipulate the symbols, even become them
and act them out when possessed, and thus understand and dominate
them, although they may consider themselves controlled by them.
Possessed individuals consider themselves to be directed by
omnipotent external forces, when in reality it is aspects of their own
personalities, developed from personal experience, which are actually
the temporary riders of the horses.

The possessing deities or spirits of a society conform to certain
general personality types commensurate with its social structure and
cultural values. People then grow up with these deities as models to
which they mold their own conscious and unconscious attitudes.
Thus the mythical system is integrated into the personalities of the
members of the community. The god personalities are created by
man in his own image, and they conform to the inclinations and
needs of men, thus a man chooses his own deity in accordance with
his needs and ideals.

The Loa, according to Huxley, not only can inhabit anyone, but do
inhabit everyone. Every pattern of muscular tension betrays some
hidden psychological attitudes, and every attitude which is allowed to
act out its emotional life to the full is a Loa (1966: 209). I concur
with this view. I believe that everyone has many behavioral
possibilities, some perhaps mutually contradictory, only some of
which are developed. There are occasions on which some of them
can be expressed, such as Carnivals, masquerade balls, or during
various altered states of consciousness stemming from alcohol, drugs,
hypnosis, etc. Some societies tacitly recognize this fact and provide
institutions in which men have the opportunity to express these
behavioral possibilities in some sort of approved and useful form. The
deity personalities in possession cults are perhaps the best cultural

institutions to provide for such self-expression to such a complete degree but still within socially and individually safe limits. Huxley notes that in Haiti there is an unacceptable, antisocial fashion in which such attitudes are expressed outside of the ritual context. This is a 'saisissement', a hysterical seizure provoked by personal upset in which the individual, completely overcome by frustrated energies, runs around madly, roaring and raging (1966: 209).

This liberation of old attitudes frequently stamps an image on the devotee (that of his deity) which links him in his normal life with the attitudes for which his normal life finds no room. The deity personality of possession is the image of these attitudes called to mind and put into action. The individual does not usually remember what happened while possessed but may recover this experience in dreams and subsequent possessions. This implies that these memories, of which each individual has many, are linked to certain kinds of attitudes and feelings and are provoked by certain specific stimuli. To recover a memory it may be necessary to recover the attitude one had when experiencing the event (Huxley 1966: 209). Huxley's ideas about memory apply to everyday experiences to some degree but are especially significant in this realm of trance and possession states, since there is a continuity of consciousness between the possession states, with lacunae in the normal states between. Only a recreation of the stimuli from the situation in which the possession personality was developed can recall the memory of this new personality to mind and evoke the appropriate behavior, all memory of which is lost when the possession attitude itself is missing. Some continuity exists because the individual is aware of who his deity is and what his characteristics are, although he may not know how he himself portrays the deity. Also there is continuity of his unconscious motivation from real life through his successive possessions, disjunctive though they may seem from superficial observation.

The training of a novice consists in ordering what was at first a confusion of parts of attitudes. The novice learns the behavior of the deity by initiation, either quite consciously or while in a state of lethargy. It would seem that after a time these more or less conscious efforts would meet the unconscious efforts to which they correspond, and real possession would take place. Out of the immense confusion of the first seizure a dominant posture or a number of different postures are disentangled, each with its own meaning and behavior, and these are the deities who possess the devotee. The possessed devotees act out rites of the relationship of men to the deities and of the deities to each other. Anyone who has been a devotee for long enough will eventually feel these relationships within himself (Huxley 1966: 210).

In the psychodrama of possession the devotee manifests his underlying or unexpressed tendencies both to himself and to others. He need not feel hesitant to do so because not he but his deity is responsible for his behavior, and also because since others are possessed by the same deities the tendencies and impulses he expresses are not unique to him but common to many people, which makes them more acceptable. Also they are expressed in culturally stylized rather than idiosyncratic form in a valuable institution where such behavior is approved and appreciated. Man is closer to the gods in going beyond the limits of behavior set by the society. It would seem that people would be healthier because of this possibility to develop and express a great deal more of the spectrum of their possible behavior than everyday life allows. They should also be relatively fulfilled and self-actualized, particularly given that many of them occupy stations in life which do not provide much self-fulfillment, which is why many people belong to such groups. They should not be frustrated at not being able to assume the roles they would like, or embarrassed at trying to do so, because such possibilities are institutionalized in religious ritual. Most participants do not play artificially imposed roles as in the theater, but act out spontaneously roles which are theirs because they come out of their own personalities. According to Douyon, people are not always possessed in the same way from one possession to the next. They may act out different facets of the same deity or different deities, where the latter is possible. In Haiti every devotee has approximately two to five Loa, mambos and houngans being receptive to an average of twenty-five (1964: 231). It is apparent then that the devotees are allowed a great range of self-expression.

It is recognized that such freedom of expression is not possible on the profane level of everyday social life. However, on the more significant sacred level where they become living gods to whom everything is permitted without question or reproach, devotees can express other sides of themselves. Given the relative status of gods and men, and men's identification with the gods they become, Bastide's thesis that social reality is a reflection of the religious structure becomes quite understandable. People see themselves most positively when they can identify themselves with these all-powerful beings which they become, when their degree of being is much increased by their participation in the essence of these divine entities. They identify with the gods and both consciously and unconsciously pattern their lives, behavior, and social interaction on the models set by them. On one level the religion is a reflection of the society because the gods' characteristics and interaction are man's projection of his social structure and cultural values. On the level of the beliefs of the people involved in the religion, however, as opposed to those of outside observers, daily life is patterned according to the mold furnished by the creators and controllers of the world. Thus in Geertz's terms, the religious system is both a model of and a model for social life (1966: 8). Which it is depends upon whether the analysis is done from an etic or emic point of view.

The various societies in question offer different degrees of possibilities for self-expression in trance and possession. In Bali there are a limited number of roles in the Witch and Dragon play — just either of the two principals and the anonymous followers. The followers, according to Belo, only report feeling anger, no other emotions (1960: 223-224). The trances and dancing of the mediums show personal style but no assumption of a totally new form of behavior. People may be possessed by masks and in some villages by animals or household items, but except in the animal impersonations they merely seem to give vent to pent-up emotions rather than to express any personal attitudes. In the animal possession people do behave like the animals, which seem usually to manifest a playful attitude, but again there is no acting out of real personal attitudes or facets of one's personality. The entranced Balinese seem to express merely general emotional qualities such as anger, dependence, playfulness, etc., the normal lack of expression of which is common and expected in Balinese society. This is commensurate with Bateson and Mead's statement that the Balinese have less sense of individual uniqueness than of identification with others. Also in most forms of trance they are not considered possessed by outside entities. In the plays they are merely acting while entranced, and the gods which possess the mediums are apparently quite impersonal.

In the religions in which the devotees are ceremonially possessed by gods and spirits who impart their personalities to them, there are also different degrees of self-expression permitted. In the traditional

Dahomean and Yoruba cults in Africa, only one deity was served by a devotee, but possession by him was not expected to allow the expression of any personal tendencies. The benefit to the devotee was mainly the opportunity to be appreciated by others in such an exalted position. In Bahia possession by a god is supposed to express a facet of the devotee's personality, but although there are many deities, an individual may, in the traditional Yoruba cults, only be possessed by one. Perhaps the devotee may enact different aspects of the same deity on different occasions, but this is not mentioned in the literature. A person may sometimes be spontaneously possessed during a ceremony by a deity that is not his own, and which represents another aspect of himself striving for expression, but this unruly Orisha is quickly sent away by the priest or priestess. Thus the freedom of the individual to express various elements of his personality is limited. This fact is probably related, in contrast to the Haitian situation, to the close ties of Bahian cults to the religious structure and mythology of their Yoruba ancestors. Also the initiation period is important and the individual only learns to worship his one deity whom he will enact in the ceremonial ritual where the lives and acts of the gods are portrayed.

In Haiti, where the religion is less organized than in Bahia, people can be possessed by deities other than the principal one for whom they have been initiated, thus they can express various facets of their personalities. Haitian rituals, as opposed to those in Bahia, are more concerned with expressing the personalities, attitudes, and tastes of the deities than with re-enacting the events of their lives, which in Haiti have been largely forgotten. Also in Haiti there are new gods who developed from the Haitian experience. The same is true in the non-traditional groups in Brazil. This is in line with the trend to less cultural determinism and more individual self-expression as the religious system becomes less organized and ceases to have control over an integrated human community.

The institution of possession appears to have very positive functions in a society for both social and individual reasons. The social value has been amply discussed and it seems quite probable that culturally controlled possession contributes positively to the good mental health of the community. More people would probably be psychologically disturbed if they did not have this culturally constituted defense mechanism to allow them to work out many of their problems. The safety of the possession institution seems to protect the individuals involved. Bowers states that individualized dissociation and the expression of multiple personalities usually represents the deterioration of the individual, whereas possession is often used to normalize the psychopathology of individuals. This is evidenced by the frequent observation of people who, in the course of hysterical or psychosomatic illnesses, are taught to channel their symptoms into approved ritual acts which normal members of the community find reassuring (Bowers 1961: 280). They may become shamans or members of possession cults designed for healing such as the Zar and the N'Deup cults. Much of the literature on possession stresses the low incidence of psychopathology in particular societies because of the institution of possession (e.g., Belo, 1960; Douyon 1964; Métraux 1958; Stainbrook 1952).

De Heusch suggests that since most researchers now no longer believe that possession is a form of hysteria, perhaps Western hysteria should be looked upon as a bad or unhappy kind of possession because it is deprived of a social frame of reference (1965: 167). Possession and hysteria seem to be different manifestations of the same basic mechanism, but whereas the one is socially approved, structured, and supported, the other is not approved or structured, and leaves the individual to suffer his dissociation in hostile surroundings. This relationship can be seen in the continuum from culturally controlled to individually expressive possession in the presence of different degrees of religious structuring.

This idea is supported by Wallace's evidence from the peyote experiment discussed in the chapter on cultural determinism. The whites, with their lack of cultural definition of the situation, had unpleasant experiences from the peyote, and their behavior tended to be not only unpleasant and disorganized, but also quite antisocial and normally unacceptable to themselves and others outside of the clinical atmosphere. The Indians, in contrast, experienced the same physiological changes with a totally different interpretation of the experience. For them it was a very positive, sacred experience in which their behavior was stylized and acceptable, and which resulted in a great feeling of well-being.

In a traditional setting with its cultural patterns and support, the individual's regression will be in the service of the ego if he follows the forms provided. Where this cultural patterning and support are lacking, such behavior will tend more toward regression proper. Thus the people in a given cultural milieu who would have a propensity for normal, approved regression in the service of the ego in a traditional religious ritual, may experience similar behavior in a non-traditional setting, but it will tend toward regression proper because of the lack of cultural patterning, support, and approval. The women in Douyon's study, for example, were conditioned as children to experience a type of behavior which was positively valued in their traditional milieu, but to which their new urban home is neither receptive nor propitious. If these women can be classified as neurotic, as Douyon says, it is for this reason. The behavior for which they developed a propensity in childhood, and for which they would be appreciated in the rural setting, is disapproved in the new setting, which also creates new problems for them which they are not equipped to resolve. The techniques they originally learned for the resolution of such problems have become dysfunctional.

There are a variety of psychological mechanisms involved in possession. The members of the culture first project their ideals and aspirations into the supernatural, personifying these qualities in anthropomorphic deities. These deities are then seen to possess their devotees, who can identify with them, and act out their behavior. This is in essence identifying with one's own ideals and aspirations and acting them out, since the deity the devotee chooses from the spectrum of possibilities is the one which most closely fits his own desires. The possession experience is cathartic in that suppressed and repressed emotions, impulses, and attitudes, can be expressed directly by the possessed people, and vicariously experienced by the spectators with no negative repercussions. Potentially neurotic or psychotic tendencies are channelled into safe behavior, as what could be regression proper is manifest as regression in the service of the ego. The possessed individual may exercise his need for dependence in renouncing all responsibility for his behavior and for his person. The gods control and are responsible for his behavior, and he depends entirely upon the priest and community of spectators to direct and take care of him. The religious system provides the major set of defense mechanisms with which individuals can resolve most of the problems and stresses created by the society.

Ludwig considers that altered states of consciousness can be adaptive or maladaptive. When they are maladaptive they have no constructive purpose and can endanger the individual or hamper his functioning in the society. They may be maladaptive when they involve, among other things, symbolic acting out of unconscious conflicts (in a socially unacceptable manner, of course), inappropriate defensive reactions in threatening, anxiety-producing situations, neurotic attempts to resolve emotional conflicts, or manifestations of self-destructive tendencies (1968: 86-89). Similar phenomena occur in possession, but in a culturally structured way that makes them adaptive. Unconscious conflicts are acted out symbolically but the symbols and means of acting out are approved and thus not considered neurotic. Even self-destructive tendencies are given positive functional significance in the personages of certain deities. They can be acted out in a controlled situation and thus not be allowed to get out of hand.

Altered states of consciousness may also be functional for the individual and the society. They may be particularly useful in healing because of the heightened suggestibility of the patient, the tendency to give increased meaning and weight to ideas, the propensity for emotional catharsis, and the frequent subsequent feeling of rejuvenation. Some altered states of consciousness aid in the maintenance of psychic equilibrium and mental health. They can also open the way to new realms of knowledge, inspiration, and religious experience. The wisdom revealed during spirit possession, for example, is believed to provide superhuman knowledge which could not be obtained with normal consciousness. High status is obtained through fulfilling a valued role in which the individual is permitted to express and relieve psychic tensions and conflicts. Both the psychological benefit and the social value help the individual to function better as a member of the community. Also the dramatic behavior in possession ceremonies serves to convince the participants of the continued personal interest of their gods in them, to reaffirm their religious beliefs, and to allow the community of men to exert some control over the unknown, all while enhancing group solidarity.

Given the concept of religious systems as both models of and models for social reality, and also the intimate relationship between the possessing deities and their devotees, it follows that both the structure and the content of possession cults reveal elements of the social structure and cultural values in both static and changing social situations. The characters and relationships of the gods among themselves reflect social reality. Huxley says, apropos of Haiti, "Ostensibly to do with the relationships between the living and the dead ... voodoo in practice is a formal set of relationships between the living themselves, which come to a head whenever a question of power arises" (1966: 132). Douyon states that in Haiti most individual conflicts are with the dead or the Loa rather than with other people. In interhuman rapport people proceed via supernatural mediation, hence the frequency of emotional problems of supernatural origin. The Haitian peasants live in great material poverty but their supernatural beliefs are much more important in the scheme of life. More disputes are concerned with people's duties to the Loa than with material problems, and the supernatural world is much more fearful than the human world (1964: 249, 251).

Huxley's statement may seem a bit exaggerated because he makes a clear distinction between the supernatural and natural worlds, whereas the Haitians do not make such a dichotomy. The supernatural beings are very much a part of everyday life and do intervene in the ordinary everyday affairs of humans. People may make deals with them to assure social or material success, and the gods in turn, if jealous or angry, may send misfortune. Thus most disputes involve the deities rather than other humans because even if other people are involved for what appear to be purely material or social reasons, the fundamental cause of the problem lies with the deities, although they may use humans as their agents, and can only be resolved by rectifying one's relationship with the offended deity. The deities are ultimately in control of every aspect of a person's life, which explains any turn of fortune, and it is they, not their human agents, who must be dealt with. In this sense, however, human relations with the deities do actually represent interhuman interaction and the attempted resolution of problems unresolvable on the social level on the supernatural, symbolic plane.

I would expect that an examination of the structure and content of possession cults would reveal a great deal about the society, revealing many of its fundamental values projected onto the supernatural plane and then seen as having an independent existence. Basic tendencies and themes of the society would probably play a large role, like the family conflict in the Balinese Witch and Dragon play. The key conflict in Haiti is perhaps the class structure and the effort to assure physical survival in unfavorable material conditions, and in the Haouka cult of the Songhay it is evidently the conflict between Songhay tradition and the Western encroachment. Harris' analysis of possession among the Taita of Kenya shows how the content and structure of this manifestation reflect sexual differences in status values, women's attitudes toward men, and the general attitude about the behavioral propensities of women (1957). I would expect the main stresses and conflicts of the society to be represented and acted out in the possession cult and resolved symbolically on this level. The powerful religious symbols involved explain all of life and provide man with a way of coping with it, so the resolution of problems on this plane is undoubtedly seen as more meaningful than their resolution on the human plane because they ultimately stem from the former. Also since human life is seen as a reflection of supernatural life, and because the deities control all aspects of human life, any rectification of man's relationships with the supernatural should have a positive effect on the well-being of both the community and the specific actors involved.

These possession cults are thus quite similar in behavioral manifestation and general significance, the elucidation and explanation of which has been the main point of this study. However, once this is established I think it is important to consider more profoundly the significance of possession in specific societies to find out what its role and function are and what it indicates about the society as a whole. It is the differences between various possession cults and types of possession which then become important. The types of possessing agents, their characteristics, and the relationships among them and between them and men, would be very revealing in both static and changing social situations.

I would expect social and cultural changes to be reflected in changes in the personalities, functions, and myths of the deities, and in the content and form of the possessions. For example, more men than women may begin to be possessed, as is true with the Haouka; individuals may be possessed by more deities than traditionally, some of them newly invented to image new experiences; the content of the interaction of the deities should change to reflect new social realities; possessions may be more violent, more playful, more artificial, etc.; and individualism should assume a generally larger role manifest in more personal self-expression and idiosyncratic possession, in contravention of the traditional norms.[1] It would be useful to observe such changes over time to understand the reactions of the people involved through their imaging of such experience. An analysis of the

---

[1] Douyon's psychological testing would have been more revealing had he related the results of the tests to the personalities of the deities incarnated by the women he tested. In this way the relationship between the women's psychological states and their socio-cultural milieu could have been made more evident.

personality characteristics, behavior, and interaction of the newly invented type two and type three possessing agents would indicate a great deal about social and cultural changes in a given society and the new values and problems involved. If possessing agents of two or all three types appear in the same ceremony, which is apparently sometimes the case (in the areas where this is possible because they all exist) the interaction between them should reveal past and present stages of the society at the same time.

BIBLIOGRAPHY

Les Afro-Américains. Mémoires de l'Institut Fondamental d'Afrique Noire, No. 27 (1953).

Bascom, William. "La Religion Africaine au Nouveau Monde," Les Religions Africaines Traditionelles (Rencontres Internationales de Bouaké). Paris: Editions du Seuil, 1965.

Bastide, Roger. Les Amériques Noires. Paris: Payot, 1967.

— —. Le Candomblé de Bahia (Rite Nâgo). Paris: Mouton & Co., 1958.

— —. Estudos Afrobrasileiros. 3rd series. Sao Paulo, 1953.

— —. "Le Messianisme chez les Noirs du Brésil," Le Monde Non-Chrétien, No. 13-16 (1950), 301-308.

— —. "Le Messianisme Raté," Archives de Sociologie des Religions, Vol. 3, No. 5 (January — June, 1958), 31-37.

— —. Les Religions Africaines au Brésil. Paris: Presses Universitaires de France, 1960.

— —. Sociologie et Psychanalyse. Paris: Presses Universitaires de France, 1950.

— —. "Le Spiritisme au Brésil," Archives de Sociologie des Religions, Vol. 24 (July—December, 1967).

— —. "Structures Sociales et Religions Afro-Brésiliennes," Renaissance, No. 2-3 (1944-45), 14-29.

Bateson, Gregory and Mead, Margaret. Balinese Character. New York: New York Academy of Sciences, 1942.

Beattie, John. Other Cultures. New York: The Free Press of Glencoe, 1964.

Belo, Jane. Trance in Bali. New York: Columbia University Press, 1960.

Benedict, Ruth. "Anthropology and the Abnormal," Journal of General Psychology, No. 10 (1934), 59-82.

Betsch, Johnnetta. The Possession Pattern in Traditional West African and New World Negro Cultures. (Unpublished Master's thesis—Northwestern University, Evanston, Ill.).

Bourguignon, Erika. "The Persistence of Folk Belief: Some Notes on Cannibalism and Zombis in Haiti," Journal of American Folklore, No. 72 (1959).

— —. "The Self, the Behavioral Environment, and the Theory of Spirit Possession," Context and Meaning in Cultural Anthropology, ed. Melford E. Spiro. New York: The Free Press, 1965.

— —, and Pettay, Louanna, "Spirit Possession, Trance and Cross Cultural Research," Symposium on New Approaches to the Study of Religion, (Proceedings of the 1964 Annual Spring Meeting of the American Ethnological Society), Seattle: University of Washington Press, 1964.

Bowers, Margaretta K., Brecher-Marer, Sylvia, and Polatin, Alvin H. "Hypnosis in the Study and Treatment of Schizophrenia—A Case Report," International Journal of Clinical and Experimental Hypnosis, No. 9 (1961), 119-138.

Bowers, Margaretta K. "Hypnotic Aspects of Haitian Voodoo," International Journal of Clinical and Experimental Hypnosis, No. 9 (1961), 269-282.

Cannon, W. B. "Voodoo Death," American Anthropologist, No. 44 (1942).

Carneiro, Edison. Candomblés da Bahia. 3rd Edition, Rio de Janeiro: Conquista, 1961.

— —. "The Structure of African Cults in Bahia," Journal of American Folklore, No. 53 (1940).

Courlander, Harold. "Dance and Dance-Drama in Haiti," The Function of the Dance in Human Society, ed. Franziska Boas. New York: The Boas School, 1944.

– –. *The Drum and the Hoe: Life and Lore of the Haitian People*. Berkeley: University of California Press, 1960.

de Heusch, Luc. "Cultes de Possession et Religions Initiatiques de Salut en Afrique," *Religions de Salut* ("Centre d'Etudes des Religions", No. 2, Brussels: Université Libre de Bruxelles, 1962).

– –. "Possession et Chamanisme – Essai d'Analyse Structurale," *Les Religions Traditionelles Africaines* ("Rencontres Internationales de Bouaké", Paris: Editions du Seuil, 1965).

Deren, Maya. *Divine Horsemen – The Living Gods of Haiti*. London: Thames and Hudson, 1953.

Derose, Rodolphe, *Caractère, Culture, Vodou: Formation et Interprétation de l'Individualité Haitienne*. Port-au-Prince: Bibliothèque Haitienne, 1956.

Devereux, George. "Normal and Abnormal; The Key Problem of Psychiatric Anthropology," *Some Uses of Anthropology: Theoretical and Applied*. Washington, D. C.: The Anthropological Society of Washington, 1956.

Douyon, Emerson. *La Crise de Possession dans le Vaudou Haitien*. (Doctoral dissertation, Université de Montreal, 1964).

– –. "La Crise de Possession dans le Vaudou Haitien," (Abstract of doctoral dissertation), *Transcultural Psychiatric Research*, Vol. 2 (October 1965), 155-159.

– –. "L'Examen au Rorschach des Vaudouisants Haitiens," *Trance and Possession States*, ed. Raymond Prince. Montreal: University of Montreal Press, 1968.

– –. "Research Model on Trance and Possession States in the Haitian Voodoo," A paper presented before the Conference on Research and Resources of Haiti (New York: The Conference, November 1-4, 1967).

Douyon, Lamarck. "Carnaval et Personalité," *Revue de la Faculté d'Ethnologie*, Université d'Etat d'Haiti, No. 13 (1968), 25-27.

Duvignand, Jean. "Existence et Possession," *Critique*, Vol. 15 (March 1959).

Eliade, Mircea. *Shamanism: Archaic Techniques of Ecstasy*. New York: Pantheon Books, 1964.

Fernandes, Gonçalves. *Xangôs do Nordeste: Investigações sôbre os Cultos Negrofetichistas do Recife*. Rio de Janeiro: Biblioteca de Divulgação Scientifica – Civilização Brasileira, S. A., 1937.

Field, Margaret J. *Religion and Medicine of the Gã People*. London: Oxford University Press, 1961.

Forde, Daryll. *The Yoruba-speaking People of Southwest Nigeria*. London: International African Institute, 1951.

Frazier, E. Franklin. "The Negro Family in Bahia, Brazil," *American Sociological Review*, Vol. 7, No. 4 (August 1942), 465-478.

Freed, Stanley A. and Ruth S. "Spirit Possession as Illness in a North Indian Village," *Magic, Witchcraft, and Curing*, ed. John Middleton. New York: The Natural History Press, 1967.

Freyre, Gilberto. *The Masters and the Slaves*. New York: Alfred A. Knopf, 1946.

Geertz, Clifford. "Religion as a Cultural System," *Anthropological Approaches to the Study of Religion*, ed. Michael Banton. London: Tavistock Publications Limited, 1966.

Gill, Merton M. and Margaret Brenman. *Hypnosis and Related States: Psychoanalytic Studies in Regression*. New York: International University Press, Inc., 1959.

Gorer, Geoffrey. "Function of Dance Forms in Primitive African Communities," *The Function of Dance in Human Society*, ed. Franziska Boas. New York: The Boas School, 1944.

Griaule, Marcel. *Dieu d'Eau – Entretiens avec Ogotemmêli*. Paris: Fayard, 1966.

Harris, Grace. "Possession 'Hysteria' in a Kenya Tribe," *American Anthropologist*, No. 59 (1957), 1046-1067.

Herskovits, Melville J. *Dahomey: An Ancient West African Kingdom.* New York: J. J. Augustin, Publisher, 1938.

— —. "Drums and Drummers in Afrobrazilian Cult Life," *The New World Negro,* ed. Frances S. Herskovits. Bloomington: Indiana University Press, 1966.

— —. *Life in a Haitian Valley.* New York: Alfred A. Knopf, 1937.

— —, and Frances S. "An Outline of Dahomean Religious Beliefs," *Memoirs of the American Anthropological Association,* No. 41, 1933.

— —. "The Social Organization of the Afrobrazilian Candomblé," *Phylon,* Vol. xvii (1956).

— —. "Some Economic Aspects of the Afrobahian Candomblé," *The New World Negro,* ed. Frances S. Herskovits, Bloomington: Indiana University Press, 1966.

— —, and Frances S. *Trinidad Village.* New York: Alfred A. Knopf, 1947.

— —. "What is Voodoo?" *The New World Negro,* ed. Frances S. Herskovits. Bloomington: Indiana University Press, 1966.

— —. "The World View of An Urban Community," *The New World Negro,* ed. Frances S. Herskovits. Bloomington: Indiana University Press, 1966.

Hoffman, Léon-François. "L'Image de la Femme dans la Poésie Haitienne", *Présence Africaine,* No. 34-35 (1960-61).

Hurston, Zora Neale. *Tell My Horse.* New York: J. B. Lippincott & Co., 1938.

Huxley, Francis. *The Invisibles: Voodoo Gods in Haiti.* New York: McGraw-Hill Book Company, 1966.

Jahn, Janheinz. *Muntu.* London: Faber & Faber, 1961.

James, William. *The Varieties of the Religious Experience.* New York: The Modern Library, 1902.

Kahn, Samuel. *Psychodrama Explained.* New York: Philosophical Library, 1964.

Kiev, Ari. "Folk Psychiatry in Haiti," *Journal of Nervous and Mental Disorders,* No. 132 (1961), 160-265.

— —. "Spirit Possession in Haiti," *American Journal of Psychiatry,* No. 118, Part 1 (1961), 133-138.

— —. "The Therapeutic Value of Spirit-Possession in Haiti," *Trance and Possession States,* ed. Raymond Prince. Montreal: University of Montreal Press, 1968.

Landes, Ruth. *The City of Women.* New York: The Macmillan Company, 1947.

— —. "A Cult Matriarchate and Male Homosexuality," *Journal of Abnormal and Social Psychology,* No. 35 (1940).

— —. "Fetish Worship in Brazil," *Journal of American Folklore,* No. 53 (1940).

Lee, S. G. "Spirit Possession among the Zulu," Unpublished paper.

Leinhardt, Godfrey. *Divinity and Experience: The Religion of the Dinka.* London: Oxford University Press, 1961.

Leiris, Michel. *La Possession et ses Aspects Théâtraux chez les Ethiopiens de Gondar.* Paris: Librairie Plon, 1958.

Lima, Vincente. *Xango.* Recife, Pernambuco: Divulgaçâo do Centro de Cultura Afro-Brasileira, 1937.

Linton, Ralph. *Culture and Mental Disorders.* Illinois: Charles C. Thomas, 1956.

Ludwig, Arnold M. "Altered States of Consciousness," *Trance and Possession States,* ed. Raymond Prince. Montreal: University of Montreal Press, 1968.

Mars, Louis. "Les Crises de Loas, les Hiéroglyphes Cinétiques, et l'Ethnodrame," *Revue de la Faculté d'Ethnologie,* Université d'Etat d'Haiti, No. 11 (1966), 22-25.

— —. *La Crise de Possession dans le Vaudou.* Port-au-Prince: Imprimerie de l'Etat, 1946.

— —. "Nouvelle Contribution à l'Etude de la Crise de Possession," *Psyché: Revue Internationale des Sciences de l'Homme et de Psychanalyse,* No. 60 (October 1951), 640-669.

— —. "La Psychopathologie du Vaudou," *Psyché: Revue Internationale des Sciences de l'Homme et de Psychanalyse*, No. 23-24 (September-October 1948), 1064-1088.

Maximilien, Louis. *Le Vaudou Haitien*. Port-au-Prince, Haiti: Imprimerie de l'Etat, 1945.

Mercier, Paul. "The Fon of Dahomey," *African Worlds*, ed. Daryll Forde. London: Oxford University Press, 1954.

Messing, Simon D. "Group Therapy and Social Status in the Zar Cult of Ethiopia," *Magic, Witchcraft, and Curing*. New York: The Natural History Press, 1967.

Métraux, Alfred. *Le Vaudou Haitien*. Paris: Gaillimard, 1958.

Mischel, Frances. "African 'Powers' in Trinidad: The Shango Cult," *Anthropological Quarterly*, Vol. 30, No. 1 (January 1957).

Mischel, Walter and Frances. "Psychological Aspects of Spirit Possession," *American Anthropologist*, No. 60 (1958).

Moreno, Jacob P. *Group Therapy and the Function of the Unconscious* (Psychodrama and Group Therapy Monographs, No. 35; New York: Beacon House, 1958).

— —, and Enneis, James M. *Hypnodrama and Psychodrama* (Psychodrama Monographs, No. 27; New York: Beacon House, 1950).

— —. *Psychodrama*. New York: Beacon House, 1946.

Neher, Andrew. "A Physiological Explanation of Unusual Behavior in Ceremonies Involving Drums," *Human Biology*, No. 34 (1962).

Oesterreich, T. K. *Possession, Demoniacal and Other, Among Primitives Races, in Antiquity, the Middle Ages, and Modern Times*. New York: University Books, 1966.

Orne, Martin T. "The Nature of Hypnosis: Artifact and Essence," *Journal of Abnormal and Social Psychology*, No. 58 (1959).

— —. "On the Social Psychology of the Psychological Experiment — With Particular Reference to Demand Characteristics and their Implications," *American Psychologist*, No. 17 (1962), 776-783.

Ortiz Fernandez, Fernando. *Hampa Afrocubana: Los Negros Brujos*. Madrid: Libreria de Fernando Fé, 1906.

Parrinder, Geoffrey. *West African Religion*. London: Epworth Press, 1961.

Price-Mars, Jean. *Ainsi Parla l'Oncle . . .* Haiti: Imprimerie de Compeigne, 1928.

Prince, Raymond. "Can the EEG Be Used in the Study of Possession States?" *Trance and Possession States*, ed. Raymond Prince. Montreal: University of Montreal Press, 1968.

Prince, Raymond (ed.). *Trance and Possession States*. Montreal: University of Montreal Press, 1968.

Ravenscroft, Kent. "Voodoo Possession: A Natural Experiment in Hypnosis," *International Journal of Clinical and Experimental Hypnosis*, No. 13 (July 1965), 157-182.

Richter, C. P. "On the Phenomenon of Sudden Death in Animals and Man," *Psychosomatic Medicine*, No. 19 (1957).

Rodrigues, Nina. *O Animismo Fetichista dos Negros Bahianos*. Rio de Janeiro: Biblioteca de Divulgação Scientifica — Civilização Brasileira, 1935.

Rouch, Jean. *La Religion et la Magie Songhay*. Paris: Presses Universitaires de France, 1960.

Rusillon, Henry. *Un Culte Dynastique avec Evocation des Morts chez les Sukalaves de Madagascar: La Tromba*. Paris: Librairie Alphonse Picard et Fils, 1912.

Samb, Makhourédia. "Le N'Deup—ou la Danse Rituelle de Possession," *Sénégal—Carrefour*, No. 2 (April 1967), 26-33.

Sarbin, Theodore R. "Contributions to Role-taking Theory: I. Hypnotic Behavior," *Psychological Review*, No. 57 (1950).

Sargant, William. *Battle for the Mind*. Maryland: Penguin Books, 1957.

Seabrook, William. *Witchcraft: Its Power in the World Today*. New York: Lancer Books, 1968.

Simpson, George. "The Belief System of Haitian Vodun," *American Anthropologist*, No. 47 (1945).

— —. "The Shango Cult in Nigeria and in Trinidad", *American Anthropologist*, No. 64 (1962).

Spiro, Melford E. "Religious Systems as Culturally Constituted Defense Mechanisms," *Context and Meaning in Cultural Anthropology*, ed. Melford E. Spiro. New York: The Free Press, 1965.

— —, and D'Andrade, Roy G. "A Cross-Cultural Study of Some Supernatural Beliefs," *American Anthropologist*, No. 60 (1958), 456-466.

Stainbrook, Edward, "Some Characteristics of the Psychopathology of Schizophrenic Behavior in Bahian Society," *American Journal of Psychiatry*, No. 109 (1952), 330-335.

Tallant, Robert. *Voodoo in New Orleans*. New York: Macmillian Company, 1946.

Tannenbaum, Frank. *Slave and Citizen*. New York: Vintage Books, 1946.

Turner, Lorenzo. "Some Contacts of Brazilian Ex-Slaves with Nigeria, West Africa," *Journal of Negro History*, No. 27 (1942), 55-67.

Turner, Victor. "Structure and Communitas," Unpublished Manuscript (1968).

Underwood, Frances W. and Honigmann, Irma. "A Comparison of Socialization and Personality in Two Simple Societies," *American Anthropologist*, No. 49 (1947).

van der Walde, Peter H. "Trance States and Ego Psychology," *Trance and Possession States*, ed. Raymond Prince. Montreal: University of Montreal Press, 1968.

Verger, Pierre. *Notes sur le Culte des Orisha et Vodun*, (Mémoires de l'Institut Fondamental d'Afrique Noire, No. 51, Dakar, Senegal, 1957).

— —. "Les Religions Traditionelles Africaines, Sont-elles Compatibles avec les Formes Actuelles de l'Existence?", *Les Religions Traditionelles Africaines* (Rencontres Internationales de Bouaké, Paris: Editions du Seuil, 1965).

— —. "Rôle Joué par l'Etat d'Hébétude au cours de l'Initiation des Novices aux Cultes des Orisha et Vodun," *Bulletin de l'Institut Fondamental d'Afrique Noire*, Série B, No. 16 (1954), 322-340.

Wallace, Anthony F. C. "Cultural Determinants of Responses to Hallucinatory Experience," *AMA Archives of General Psychiatry*, No. 1 (1959).

— —. *Culture and Personality*. New York: Random House, 1961.

— —. "Mental Illness, Biology, and Culture," *Psychological Anthropology*, ed. Francis L. K. Hsu. Illinois: The Dorsey Press, Inc., 1961.

— —. *Religion: An Anthropological View*. New York: Random House, 1966.

Walter, V. G. and W. Grey. "The Central Effects of Rhythmic Sensory Stimulation," *Electroencephalography and Clinical Neurophysiology*, No. 1 (1949), 57-86.

White, Robert. "A Preface to the Theory of Hypnotism", *Journal of Abnormal and Social Psychology*, No. 39 (1941), 477-505.

Wittkower, E. D. "Spirit Possession in Haitian Vodun Ceremonies," *Acta Psychotherapeutica et Psychosomatica*, No. 12 (1964).

Zaretsky, Irvine I. *Bibliography of Spirit Possession and Spirit Mediumship*. Evanston: Northwestern University Press, 1966.